Making Team Dynamics Visible

A Neuro-Linguistic Enneagram Approach to Unlocking Team Performance

Tang Seok Hian

Candid Creation Publishing

First published February 2025

Candid Creation Publishing books are available through most major bookstores in Singapore. For bulk order of our books at special quantity discounts, please email us at enquiry@candidcreation.com.

MAKING TEAM DYNAMICS VISIBLE

A NEURO-LINGUISTIC ENNEAGRAM APPROACH TO UNLOCKING TEAM PERFORMANCE

Author : Tang Seok Hian
Publisher : Phoon Kok Hwa
Editor : Patricia Ng
Cover designer : Ryanne Ng
Layout : Corrine Teng
Published by : Candid Creation Publishing LLP
167 Jalan Bukit Merah
#05-12 Connection One Tower 4
Singapore 150167
Website : www.candidcreation.com
Facebook : www.facebook.com/CandidCreationPublishing
Email : enquiry@candidcreation.com

National Library Board, Singapore Cataloguing-in-Publication Data

Name(s): Tang , Seok Hian.

Title: Making team dynamics visible : a neuro-linguistic enneagram approach to unlocking team performance / Tang Seok Hian.

Description: Singapore : Candid Creation Publishing LLP, 2025.

Identifier(s): ISBN 978-981-17667-1-8 (paperback)

Subject(s): LCSH: Teams in the workplace. | Neurolinguistic programming. | Enneagram.

Classification: DDC 658.4022 --dc23

PRAISE FOR *MAKING TEAM DYNAMICS VISIBLE*

"*Making Team Dynamics Visible* is an invaluable resource for leaders navigating the complexities of rapid growth and diverse team dynamics. Through the Neuro-Linguistic Enneagram (NLE) model, this book provides practical tools like the Team Map and adaptive team responses, enabling teams to uncover hidden patterns and create stronger alignment.

Leading a fast-paced, multicultural team across the region, I've witnessed first-hand how these principles help address critical challenges in communication, accountability, and trust. Seok Hian's insightful frameworks and real-world case studies make this a must-read for leaders striving to build cohesive, high-performing teams in today's ever-evolving organisational landscape."

— **Karl Mak**
CEO of Hepmil Media Group

"As an entrepreneur, I found the NLE methodology invaluable for assessing myself, my management team, and our organisation as a whole. Self-awareness is the foundation of a successful team, and this approach provides key insights into individual and team dynamics, ultimately leading to greater efficiency and collaboration. I highly recommend this book to leaders, co-founders, and managers seeking to build and lead more effective teams."

— **Bryan Oh**
CEO of NEU Battery Materials

Making Team Dynamics Visible is a much needed read for anyone that strives to be a better leader for his or her team, family, and life. It is a true exploration of the often unseen forces shaping team performance and cohesion. By combining psychological insights, practical tools like the NLE Team Profile, and actionable strategies, the book empowers leaders to understand dynamics and make sense of them to further enhance their teams and performances. A must-read for leaders, HR professionals, and team coaches seeking to make a tangible impact on team health and organisational outcomes.

— **Althea Lim**
CEO of Gushcloud International

"*Making Team Dynamics Visible* is a must-read for leaders, coaches, and facilitators seeking to unlock team potential. Blending Enneagram wisdom with modern team leadership, Seok Hian offers a powerful lens to decode and optimise team performance. In my work coaching and facilitating teams across diverse industries, I have seen first-hand how the NLE Team Model is a game changer, making the invisible forces of team dynamics tangible, transforming collaboration and performance, and turning dysfunction into flow. This book is both insightful and practical—a road map for creating teams that thrive. If you work with teams, whether as a leader, coach, or facilitator, this book belongs on your shelf."

— **Joanne Teh, MCC**
Coach | Facilitator | Trainer | Passionate about unlocking team potential

"Seok Hian's *Making Team Dynamics Visible* is a compelling and practical guide for anyone seeking to understand and apply the Enneagram in team settings. Whether you are new to the Enneagram or an experienced practitioner, this book offers valuable insights into self-awareness, leadership, and team dynamics. With a clear distinction between "reactive", "responsive", and "regenerative" types of team health, Seok Hian highlights how disengagement and conflict often stem from a lack of understanding and connection. By leveraging the Enneagram, individuals and teams can foster deeper empathy, enhance collaboration, and build trust. This book serves as an accessible yet profound resource for leaders, professionals, and anyone looking to cultivate stronger, more cohesive teams through a deeper understanding of human behaviours and collective tendencies."

— **Lay Tay**
Head of HR | Certified Coach

CONTENTS

CONTENTS

ACKNOWLEDGMENTS

There are many people who have contributed to the development of ideas and thoughts in the book, and I hope to acknowledge most of them.

I want to express my gratitude to all the Enneagram teachers, notably Ginger Lapid-Bodga, Jerome Wagner, and Peter O'Hanrahan, for their contributions to the Enneagram world and whom I had the privilege to learn from when they were conducting programmes in Singapore. I am also grateful to the Mind Transformations team and community, especially Agnes Lau, Barney Wee, and Joseph Ch'ng for their guidance and support in my own Enneagram journey, and for making the development of Neuro-Linguistic Enneagram (NLE) possible.

I would also like to express my gratitude to all my clients who have allowed me to work with them and their teams through consulting, training, or coaching, and giving me their valuable feedback on how I have supported and contributed to their teams and leadership development.

I would also like to thank my friends and partners—especially Ian Lye, Bernard Chwee, and Xiaowei Ang—as well as the

Enneagram community for their perspectives, challenges, and ideas that have enriched my understanding of Enneagram, teams, and leadership and made this book possible. Last but not least, my dearest family for their unwavering support in all my years of work.

FOREWORD

I am genuinely excited to introduce you to the Neuro-Linguistic Enneagram (NLE) Team Model, developed by ardent Enneagram practitioner Tang Seok Hian. Having known Seok Hian for over two decades, I have witnessed how she has embodied Enneagram knowledge and wisdom, transforming herself, her relationships, and her work in consulting, training, and coaching.

In this book, Seok Hian distils her vast knowledge and experience in organisations across different industries, sizes and cultures, to unveil rich insights and practical strategies for optimising team dynamics for enhanced performance. To create this groundbreaking NLE Team Model, I have seen her iterating and even discarding earlier versions, showing her commitment to develop a framework that is both profound and accessible. The Team Map, 4 Pivotal Points Spectrums, Team Health, Leadership and Team Dynamic, and Team Neuro-Actionables are all Seok Hian's innovations, which we are now so fortunate to be able to access and use.

The NLE Team Model is highly practical, and you can experience its real-world applicability in her compelling case studies. These showcase its efficacy in diverse settings. Her approach combines the introspective elements of the Enneagram with pragmatic strategies from Neuro-Linguistic Programming (NLP) together with her direct work experience of deciphering patterns in teams and leadership. It is truly transformative, unlocking doors to clearer and authentic communication, more robust collaboration, flourishing synergy and extraordinary leadership.

What I admire about Seok Hian is her unwavering dedication to empowering others, her generous sharing of knowledge and experience, and her ability to collaborate with empathy. She has presented a master class reflecting her passion for making team dynamics visible, cultivating corporate human resources to be productive and nurturing. Let yourself be guided by a true pioneer who will redefine the way you perceive effective teamwork and leadership.

Agnes Lau
Co-developer of Neuro-Linguistic Enneagram, with Tang Seok Hian and Joseph Ch'ng;

Co-author of *Choices of Now*, with Barney Wee

INTRODUCTION

My interest in working with teams started when I was part of a regional team as a team member. I was the regional Human Resources (HR) Director in a media agency, reporting to an inspiring Regional Chief Executive Officer (CEO), and worked alongside brilliant peers, and had a supportive HR team in each country within my region. Those were the most fun, exciting, and memorable years of my corporate career. None of us on the team was perfect—in fact, we each had our quirks and idiosyncrasies, and we challenged (disagreed with) each other often—but we had such a good dynamic built on trust and relationships. This first-hand experience made me believe in teams and leadership, how teams work, and how optimising team dynamics might be equally important in developing individuals and leaders.

The last decade as a consultant, coach, and trainer gave me more opportunities to work with teams across different industries and organisations, ranging from start-ups, and small and medium enterprises (SMEs), to multinational corporations (MNCs). Being a practitioner, I analysed and learnt from my direct working experience in those moments and started seeing patterns and tendencies that existed within teams, across teams, and between teams and their leaders. With the lens of Enneagram (a wonderful profiling tool that crossed my path almost 20 years back), I was able to make team dynamics visible and let teams talk about their team profiles, thus accelerating team understanding and alignment—the foundations of team performance.

Teams are the fundamental building blocks of any successful organisation, representing a dynamic amalgamation of diverse personalities, skill sets, and perspectives. However, within this intricate web of interdependencies lies the complex tapestry of team dynamics. The intricate nature of team dynamics encompasses a multitude of factors—intrapersonal, interpersonal, and the environment that the team operates in—shaping the very essence of a team's performance and success.

In this book, we embark on a journey to explore the intricacies of team dynamics and how the NLE Team Model serves as a powerful lens through which these dynamics can be understood, decoded, and optimised. Through a careful examination of the Team Map, the 4PP Spectrum, and the adaptive team responses, we uncover practical strategies and insights that will empower teams to achieve their utmost potential and drive success.

HOW TO USE THIS BOOK

The sequence of the book is as follows:

- Chapters 1 and 2 introduce Team Dynamics and Enneagram in general.
- Chapters 3 to 5 elaborate on the NLE Team Model and how different team dynamics would manifest in different states of team health.

- Chapter 6 explains the impact of leadership in team dynamics, and why we feel that a leader's profile should be separately considered to deepen the understanding of the team profile.
- Chapter 7 highlights the Neuro-Actionables unique to the NLE Team Model and ways to improve the team dynamics.
- Chapters 8 to 12 illustrate the various applications of using the NLE Team Profiles and how they enable the effectiveness of organisational interventions. Each application is presented in the form of a case study from past, real engagements. The scenarios, characters, and names of people and companies are edited to protect confidentiality and privacy.

This is a book for practitioners, by a practitioner. It is my little contribution to the Enneagram community by putting forth my practical work experiences with teams, hoping to spark more discussions, applications, and contributions regarding Enneagram team-related work. Here are a couple of things to take note of when reading this book:

- This book assumes that the readers have sufficient knowledge and familiarity with the Enneagram. Although an introduction of the general nine types will be covered, it does not do justice to the breadth and depth of work in the actual Enneagram world. Readers new to the Enneagram are encouraged to follow the book's chapters in sequence to build their understanding progressively and to refer to more information through other Enneagram books and websites. Enneagram practitioners who are experienced working with teams, however, may begin directly with Chapter 3 to explore the NLE methodology. For Chapters 8 to 12, readers can select case studies of interest without adhering to a sequential reading order.

- This book uses the Neuro-Linguistic Enneagram (NLE) profiling tool that I co-developed with Mind Transformations Pte Ltd, based on the NLE Team Model I created, hence there may be other insights (such as the 4PP Spectrums) that other Enneagram profilers are unable to provide. Nevertheless, there will be sufficient illustrations on how you can apply the Enneagram in team settings given any of the Enneagram tools out there.

Please join me on this journey to make team dynamics visible and unlock the secrets to fostering a truly high-performing and effective team.

Chapter 1

INTRODUCTION TO TEAM DYNAMICS

WHAT IS TEAM DYNAMICS?

Team dynamics refer to the psychological forces that emerge from the interplay of individual personalities and roles within a group or team setting. It encompasses the patterns of communication, cooperation, and tensions that shape the overall functioning and effectiveness of a team. It is also commonly known as "politics"—especially when the dynamic gets in the way and work is undermined. In the wonderful book, *An Everyone Culture*, authors Robert Kegan and Lisa Lahey talked about the "second job" that everyone in corporate is doing that nobody is paying them for.[1] In my perspective, this is part of the team dynamics that I wish to uncover and reveal, hoping to make this visible enough for teams to have deeper conversations that build understanding and trust.

Research on team dynamics underscores the significance of understanding the complex interrelationships between team members, the influence of leadership styles, and the impact of group norms and cohesion on team performance. According to Richard Hackman and Ruth Wageman's influential research, team dynamics are not just the aggregate of individual behaviours, but rather the emergent properties that result from the interaction of team members pursuing a common goal.[2] Moreover, Meredith Belbin's seminal work on team roles highlights the importance of recognising the diversity of roles within a team and the impact of role interdependence on team dynamics and performance.[3] Bruce Tuckman's model of group development also emphasises the stages of forming, storming, norming, and performing, shedding light on the evolving nature of team dynamics as groups progress toward achieving their objectives.[4]

---

1 Kegan, Robert, and Lisa Laskow Lahey. *An Everyone Culture: Becoming a Deliberately Developmental Organization.* Boston, MA: Harvard Business School Publishing, 2016.

2 Hackman, J. Richard, and Ruth Wageman. "When and How Team Leaders Matter." *Research in Organizational Behavior: An Annual Series of Analytical Essays and Critical Reviews, Vol 26*, edited by Barry Staw and Roderick M. Kramer, Oxford, UK: JAI Press, 2005, pp. 37–74.

3 Belbin, R. Meredith. *Management Teams: Why They Succeed or Fail.* London, UK: Heinemann, 1981.

4 Tuckman, Bruce W. "Developmental Sequence in Small Groups." *Psychological Bulletin*, vol. 63, no. 6, 1965, p. 384.

Contemporary research post-2000 by Michael West's team effectiveness framework emphasises the critical role of interpersonal processes, such as communication, trust, and collaboration, in shaping positive team dynamics and facilitating innovation and productivity.[5] Additionally, the growing importance of psychological safety and emotional intelligence within teams, as proposed by Cary Cherniss and Daniel Goleman[6] as well as Amy Edmondson[7,8] highlights the essential role of building emotional awareness, emotional regulation, and trust in fostering constructive team dynamics and effective decision-making.

Understanding the intricacies of team dynamics is crucial for optimising team performance and fostering a collaborative work environment. However, despite the abundance of diverse team models and leadership frameworks, the realisation of optimal team performance and successes continues to be left to chance, indicating **a persistent gap** in effectively unlocking a team's potential.

I have had my fair share of experiences working in teams—both as a team member and a team leader—and working with teams across levels (from C-suites to operational teams), organisational

5 West, Michael A. *Effective Teamwork: Practical Lessons from Organizational Research*. 3rd ed., West Sussex, UK: British Psychological Society and John Wiley & Sons, Ltd, 2012.

6 Cherniss, Cary, and Daniel Goleman, editors. *The Emotionally Intelligent Workplace: How to Select for, Measure, and Improve Emotional Intelligence in Individuals, Groups, and Organizations.* San Francisco, CA: Jossey-Bass, 2001.

7 Edmondson, Amy. "Psychological Safety and Learning Behavior in Work Teams." *Administrative Science Quarterly*, vol. 44, no. 2, 1999, pp. 350–383.

8 Edmondson, Amy C. *How Organizations Learn, Innovate, and Compete in the Knowledge Economy.* San Francisco, CA: Jossey-Bass, 2012.

sizes (from start-ups to large enterprises), and industries. As a consultant, trainer, and leadership coach, I have participated in and contributed to varying degrees of organisational changes, depending on the scope of engagement. When a team is not performing, it often surfaces as a "communication issue"—ranging from people having side conversations, miscommunication, and misunderstandings, to confrontational conflicts and apathetic "silent treatments"—deep down, it usually narrows down to four common "causes":

- Structural Issues

  This includes the inherent "check-and-balance" that an organisation is set out to create and it can create "conflicts" and "misunderstandings", such as the Finance team is supposed to control Marketing costs, and the Internal Audit division is meant to challenge every other division. Other structural effects include matrix team structures that can easily lead to a lack of trust and misaligned communication.
- Systems and Process Issues

  This includes a lack of, or inefficient, systems and processes that hinder productivity. Strong bureaucracy can also result in frustrations and transactional work relationships. Inconsistent systems and processes can cause misunderstandings and make people feel "questioned" when errors occur.
- Competency Issues

  This includes the skills and abilities within the team, including those of the team leader. A general lack of communication skills can also contribute to poor team performance; however, this is often more of a symptom than a cause. Other common skills-based challenges include not knowing how to collaborate, overly narrow skills, and general poor management skills.

- Relational Issues

  This includes a lack of trust and understanding within the team; emotional baggage from the past, unresolved conflicts; unresourceful individuals (e.g. low self-awareness, toxic or difficult personalities, etc.); and not having the time to build personal relations (e.g. everyone working remotely or an influx of new hires due to attrition).

All these experiences have enriched my understanding and passion for improving team dynamics and effectiveness. One trend that became clear to me was that there is a growing need to instil leadership into the whole team, and not fix the team leader alone.

LEADERSHIP VERSUS LEADER

In today's fast-paced and ever-evolving work environments, it is not possible to expect the leader to "know-it-all", hence over the years, decision-making authority has shifted from a centralised to decentralised model. In the VUCA (volatile, uncertain, complex, and ambiguous) world, leaders even need to be comfortable making decisions without sufficient information and take on an agile or iterative approach toward problem-solving.

As the concept of work changes, the types of teams and the frequency of team formations have changed as well. Many teams are now made up of different "types of members"—some are employed by the organisation while others are contracted externally (including freelancers)—with varying degrees of "control" and different types of engagement. While the team leader may be responsible for the overall team performance, the dynamics are influenced and impacted by every "member" of the team.

When I was a corporate HR professional, I had heard of employees leaving the organisation or seeking role transfers to another department due to the current team being "too political". In addition to the diversity of the personalities in a team, a group of highly competent individuals does not naturally lead to a high-performing team. In his book, *The Fifth Discipline*, Peter Senge posed the question, "How can a team of committed managers with individual IQs above 120 have a collective IQ of 63?"[9] A part of the answer is on how healthy the team is.

Although a standardised definition of team health remains elusive, most people would be able to give you some behavioural evidence when a team is "healthy" or "unhealthy". A "healthy" or functional team is likely to have productive meetings, effective work relations, and constructive feedback and accountability conversations. An "unhealthy" or dysfunctional team often has meetings that have skewed participation (e.g. silent members or dominated by a few individuals), recycled agendas, and many side conversations outside formal channels. While the leader typically has the formal authority to make the biggest impact on team health, this is not the exclusive ability and ownership of the team leader. As such, everyone has the opportunity and responsibility to make a team healthy. I will expound more about Team Health in Chapter 4.

---

9 Senge, Peter M. *The Fifth Discipline: The Art and Practice of the Learning Organization*. New York, NY: Crown Publishing Group, 2010.

In summary, the need for a more systemic yet comprehensive approach to decode and reveal these team dynamics has become increasingly evident. Organisations must embrace holistic approaches that go beyond superficial understanding, delving deep into the underlying layers of team interactions to unlock the true abilities of a team.

Chapter 2

INTRODUCTION TO ENNEAGRAM

BRIEF HISTORY AND DEVELOPMENT OF THE ENNEAGRAM

Originating from ancient wisdom traditions, the Enneagram integrates modern psychological insights, offering a profound understanding of the intricacies of human personality and the underlying patterns that drive our thoughts, emotions, and actions.

One of the earliest documented instances of the Enneagram in the modern context can be attributed to the teachings of George Ivanovich Gurdjieff, a spiritual teacher and mystic, in the early

20th century (1920s). Gurdjieff used the Enneagram as a symbol to represent various universal laws and processes, incorporating it into his teachings on human consciousness and self-awareness.

In the latter half of the 20th century (1950s), Oscar Ichazo, a Bolivian psychologist and mystic, further developed the Enneagram system, emphasising its psychological applications and its potential for personal growth and transformation. Ichazo's work laid the foundation for the Enneagram's integration into contemporary psychology and spirituality.

Later, Claudio Naranjo, a Chilean psychiatrist, introduced the Enneagram to the field of psychology and personal development (1970s), popularising it as a tool for self-discovery and understanding human behaviour. Naranjo's contributions expanded the Enneagram's application beyond spiritual contexts, making it accessible to a broader audience interested in personal growth, relationships, and psychological well-being.

At its core, the Enneagram identifies nine distinct personality types, each characterised by specific core motivations, fears, desires, and behavioural patterns. These nine types form interconnected points on a geometric figure (see figure 2.1), symbolising the interrelatedness and interdependence of human personalities. Through its rich and nuanced framework, the Enneagram serves as a powerful tool for self-discovery, personal growth, and fostering deeper insights into interpersonal dynamics and relationships.

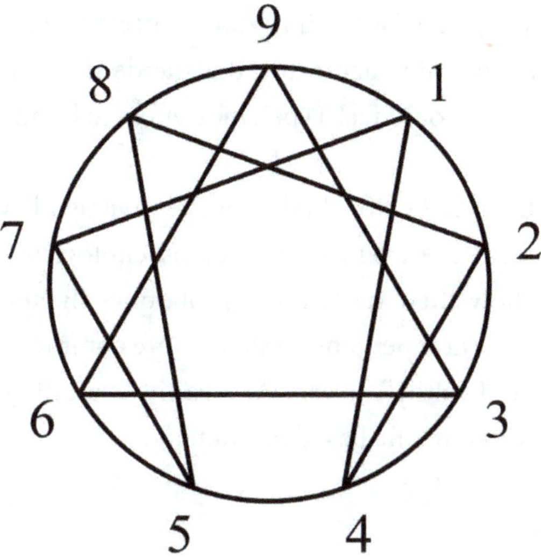

Figure 2.1: The Enneagram.

ENNEAGRAM NINE TYPES OVERVIEW

The Enneagram that we use today was developed in the 1970s, infused with modern psychology, and is a personality system that identifies nine distinct psychological structures and drives—each with its own behavioural traits, emotional patterns, and mental patterns. These nine types reflect the different ways individuals perceive the world, react emotionally, and manage their inner motivations. In this section is a brief introduction to each of the nine types.

As we study each Enneagram Type, it is important to understand that most of these are "labels" and most of them are given by people other than that Type. For example, most Type Ones would not perceive themselves to be "perfectionists" but instead, they were merely trying to get things done correctly. However, other types might not value achieving the standards valued by Type Ones and hence would feel Type Ones' effort to be an "overdrive".

The traits described below highlight the "Average Level" of each type. People at the average level of psychological health and awareness show their traits more pronouncedly and distinctly. People of different types tend to share more commonalities when they are very "healthy" or very "unhealthy", resulting in it being harder to type someone based on traits.

Type One

Type Ones are commonly labelled as "Perfectionists" or "Reformers" for their relentless drive to make things better, continuous improvements, and discernment.

- Behavioural Traits

  Type One individuals are principled, disciplined, and strive for improvement. They are organised and responsible and tend to set high standards for themselves and others. Often, they show a strong sense of duty, structure, and an inclination to correct what they see as wrong.
- Emotional Patterns

  Type Ones often experience a constant internal pressure to do things right, which can lead to frustration and disappointment when reality doesn't match their ideals. They suppress anger (known as "resentment"), feeling it's wrong to express their dissatisfaction outwardly.

- Mental Patterns

  Their thought patterns revolve around what is "right" and "wrong". Ones mentally critique themselves and others, often focusing on how things could be improved. They aim for perfection and clarity and may struggle with accepting reality.

Type Two

Type Twos are commonly labelled as "Helpers" or "Givers" due to their tendency to support and engage others in an indirect manner in order to elicit a favourable response.

- Behavioural Traits

  Type Twos are warm, generous, and highly attuned to the needs of others. They are empathetic and people-pleasing and often sacrifice their own needs to ensure the well-being of others. They thrive in relationships and are often seen as nurturing and supportive.

- Emotional Patterns

  Twos are driven by a desire to be loved and appreciated. They feel valuable when they are helping others but may also struggle with feelings of unworthiness or rejection if their efforts are not reciprocated. They may experience hidden pride in their ability to give but also an underlying fear of being unlovable.

- Mental Patterns

  They mentally focus on what others need, sometimes at the expense of their own needs. They often think about how they can earn love through acts of service and can feel hurt or rejected if they are not acknowledged or appreciated in return.

Type Three

Type Threes are commonly labelled as "Achievers" or "Performers" for their result-focused mindset, assertion to achieve their goals, and workaholism.

- Behavioural Traits

  Type Threes are goal-oriented, success-driven, and image-conscious. They are highly efficient, adaptable, and often present a polished, competent front. They focus on achieving tangible results and are excellent at marketing themselves.
- Emotional Patterns

  Threes derive their self-worth from external validation and accomplishments. They may struggle with feelings of emptiness if they fail to live up to their internal standards of success or if they sense they are not admired or valued. Deep down, they fear failure and worthlessness.
- Mental Patterns

  Their minds are constantly working toward efficiency, goals, and accomplishments. Threes think about how to achieve the next success, optimise performance, and present themselves in a way that wins approval and admiration from others.

Type Four

Type Fours are commonly labelled as "Individualists" or "Romantics" for their emotional expressions, drive to be unique, and seek for meaning.

- Behavioural Traits

  Type Fours are creative, introspective, and emotionally sensitive. They often feel unique or different from others and long for deep emotional connections. They often express themselves artistically or creatively and tend to focus on their inner emotional world.

- Emotional Patterns

  Fours experience a wide range of emotions, often feeling melancholic, longing, or envy when they perceive others as having something they lack. They frequently feel misunderstood or unappreciated, leading to a sense of longing for something elusive.

- Mental Patterns

  Fours mentally dwell on what is missing in their lives or how they are different from others. They focus on identity and personal significance, sometimes idealising the past or fantasising about a future where they are fully understood and appreciated.

Type Five

Type Fives are commonly labelled as "Observers" or "Thinkers" due to their tendency to make sense of things, go deep into a body of knowledge, and preference for solitude.

- Behavioural Traits

  Type Fives are analytical, curious, and private. They are intellectually driven, seeking to understand the world through observation and research. They tend to conserve their energy and prefer to retreat into their minds rather than engage emotionally.

- Emotional Patterns

  Fives fear being overwhelmed by their environment or relationships. They often detach from emotions and may struggle with feelings of inadequacy or depletion. Their emotional world is tightly controlled, and they may feel safer in isolation.

- Mental Patterns

  They think in terms of gathering knowledge and maintaining autonomy. They have a mental habit of detaching from emotions and external demands to preserve their inner resources. They compartmentalise and constantly analyse situations, often feeling that they need more knowledge or preparation before engaging fully.

Type Six

Type Sixes are commonly labelled as "Loyalists" or "Sceptics" for their vigilant minds, team orientation, and antagonistic yet doubtful stance.

- Behavioural Traits

  Type Sixes are loyal, responsible, and security-oriented. They value safety, structure, and predictability and are often cautious, scanning their environment for potential threats. They build strong, supportive relationships and can be excellent team players.

- Emotional Patterns

  Sixes often feel anxiety, manifesting as doubt or fear of uncertainty. They seek reassurance and support from others but may also feel suspicious or mistrustful of authority. They experience a push-pull dynamic between seeking security and questioning the very systems that provide it.

- Mental Patterns

  Their thoughts revolve around worst-case scenarios and planning for potential problems. They tend to overthink decisions, seeking certainty, and reassurance from others or external authorities. They may also question whether they can trust their own judgement.

Type Seven

Type Sevens are commonly labelled as "Enthusiasts" and "Adventurers" due to their tendency to pursue new experiences, value possibilities, and restlessness.

- Behavioural Traits

  Type Sevens are energetic, spontaneous, and fun-loving. They are enthusiastic and constantly seek new experiences and opportunities. They avoid pain and discomfort by keeping themselves busy with pleasurable or stimulating activities.

- Emotional Patterns

  Sevens often avoid negative emotions by staying focused on the positive and future possibilities. They fear being trapped in emotional pain or boredom, so they tend to distract themselves with excitement and novelty. This can lead to anxiety when they feel restricted or unable to escape.

- Mental Patterns

  Sevens mentally focus on future plans and possibilities, often jumping from one idea to another. They avoid thinking about difficult emotions or limitations by imagining new opportunities. Their minds are always racing, seeking the next adventure or distraction.

Type Eight

Type Eights are commonly labelled as "Challengers" or "Bosses" for their strong energy and tendency to dominate, assert, and impose.

- Behavioural Traits

  Type Eights are assertive, strong-willed, and protective. They value control, autonomy, and honesty, often taking charge of situations and standing up for themselves and others. They can be confrontational but also deeply caring and protective of those they deem vulnerable.
- Emotional Patterns

  Eights fear vulnerability and being controlled by others. They often suppress softer emotions, like sadness, and may express anger more readily as a way to maintain power. Eights are driven by a need to protect themselves and their loved ones, fearing weakness or betrayal.
- Mental Patterns

  Their mental focus is on power, control, and justice. Eights think in terms of protecting their boundaries and ensuring that they are not manipulated or taken advantage of. They may also focus on how to assert their will or dominate people and situations to avoid vulnerability.

Type Nine

Type Nines are commonly labelled as "Peacemakers" or "Mediators" for their tendency to go with the flow, unassuming personas, and ability to see similarities more than differences.

- Behavioural Traits

  Type Nines are easy-going, accommodating, and conflict-averse. They prioritise harmony and seek to maintain peace both internally and externally. Nines often merge with others' agendas and avoid asserting their own needs to prevent conflict.

- Emotional Patterns

  Nines suppress their own desires and preferences to avoid creating tension. This can lead to feelings of inertia or internalised frustration as they struggle to assert themselves. They often experience numbness or dissociation from their own emotions, preferring a state of calm.
- Mental Patterns

  They tend to mentally check out or "space out" as a way to avoid discomfort. They focus on keeping things comfortable and can be indecisive or passive in their thinking. Nines may have difficulty prioritising their own opinions or goals and instead focus on maintaining peace and equilibrium.

For details on how to obtain a personal profile analysis, please contact: **info@nlpsgasia.com**.

APPLICATIONS OF THE ENNEAGRAM

While the Enneagram started to be a gateway for spiritual development, over the last few decades, it now has a wider range of applications across personal development, relationships, leadership, and organisational growth. Its depth as a personality system allows individuals and groups to better understand their motivations, emotional patterns, and behaviours, making it useful in various contexts. The following are some key areas where the Enneagram is applied.

- Personal Development and Self-Awareness

  The Enneagram helps individuals gain deeper self-awareness by identifying core motivations, emotional triggers, and habitual thought patterns. It provides a framework for personal growth, allowing people to recognise unhealthy behaviours and work toward more positive expressions of their type.

- Relationships
  In relationships, the Enneagram improves communication by fostering empathy and understanding of different perspectives. It aids in conflict resolution by revealing underlying motivations, and it deepens emotional connections by offering insight into each person's relational dynamics.
- Leadership and Team Development
  Leaders use the Enneagram to enhance their leadership style, improve team collaboration, and manage conflict. It helps in identifying strengths and blind spots within teams, leading to better decision-making and increased accountability in a cohesive work environment.
- Organisational and Corporate Settings
  In corporate settings, the Enneagram is used for hiring, talent development, and improving workplace culture. It helps organisations understand employee motivations, facilitates change management, enhances productivity, and fosters a supportive, empathetic work culture.
- Coaching and Therapy
  The Enneagram is a powerful tool in life coaching and therapy, helping clients uncover deep emotional patterns and overcome limitations. It supports personal transformation, career alignment, and healing through targeted guidance and self-reflection.
- Spiritual Growth
  The Enneagram offers a pathway for spiritual development, encouraging individuals to explore the ego, false self, and deeper aspects of their spiritual energies. It's widely used in

spiritual direction and personal reflection to promote inner growth and self-realisation.

- Parenting and Family Dynamics

  Parents use the Enneagram to understand their parenting style and their children's personalities and tailor their parenting approach. It improves family communication, resolves conflicts, and fosters greater harmony by appreciating the different motivations and emotional needs of family members.

- Education and Teaching

  Educators apply the Enneagram to recognise diverse learning styles and adapt teaching methods accordingly. It enhances student engagement and helps students develop self-awareness, improving both their academic performance and personal growth.

- Health and Wellness

  The Enneagram aids mental health by identifying emotional triggers and stress points, offering strategies for managing anxiety and improving well-being. It also helps individuals achieve better work-life balance by understanding their tendencies and creating healthier habits.

- Performing Arts

  Scriptwriters, producers, directors, and actors use the Enneagram to understand and immerse themselves into the characters' development in movie plots, and how to express the psychological tendencies of the character types as the stories unfold.

UTILISATIONS PRESUPPOSITIONS OF THE ENNEAGRAM

Given such a powerful body of knowledge, it is important to use it appropriately. I often joked that if one becomes more limited after learning Enneagram (e.g. you start to feel that you can only work with certain Types), then likely one has learnt it the wrong way. From my personal experience, the Enneagram has liberated me in all my relationships—it has helped me understand and be more resourceful in all my interactions with others.

There are a few utilisation presuppositions of the Enneagram that will optimise the use of this knowledge.

- The Enneagram does not put us in a box; it shows us "the box we are already in" and the way out.
- No single Type is better or worse than any other. Therefore, the Enneagram is NOT what you like or dislike; it's about finding and accepting who you are.
- The best person to discover your Enneagram Type is yourself, through patient self-observation and studying. A profiling questionnaire may help you narrow your possible Types but you need to validate the profile results with honest self-observation.
- No one is of a "pure Type", although there is only one Core Type of motivation. Do NOT use one language, cognitive, or motivation pattern to profile a person; that pattern may be shared by several Types.
- You have one "Home" Type (Core Type), one or two "Neighbouring" dispositions (Wings), and two personality "Health" indicator qualities (Lines). The Enneagram is systematic rather than chaotic.

- Depending on the personality "Health" of two people with the same Type, they can be seen displaying very different personalities.
- Being compassionate and using other Types to understand yourself is the first place to start using the Enneagram, rather than trying to tell others how much you know about them.

We can tap into each Type's resources, through awareness, modelling, and practice.

The above presuppositions allow us to see beyond behavioural traits and jump to conclusions about one's own or other's Types. Personality is complex, and therefore it is important for us to encourage compassion in the process of growth.

OTHER CONCEPTS ABOUT THE ENNEAGRAM

Many professionals and practitioners have built on the Enneagram basic types and expounded on its richness. Below are some of the common, established concepts of Enneagram in the current Enneagram world, and growing.

Instinctual Subtypes (Instincts)

There are three instinctual subtypes based on basic human survival instincts:

- Self-preservation Subtype

  Focused on personal safety, comfort, and well-being. These individuals prioritise security, health, and their physical environment.

- Social Subtype
  Focused on group dynamics, relationships, and social roles. They are more concerned with fitting in, contributing, and being part of a community.
- Sexual (One-to-One) Subtype
  Focused on intense connections, intimacy, and personal impact. They seek deeper, often one-on-one relationships and experiences.

These instincts overlay the core Enneagram Types, creating nuanced versions of each Type, thus further dividing into twenty-seven subtypes.

Wings

Each Enneagram Type has two adjacent Types that act as "wings". These wings influence the Core Type, adding nuance, complexity, and resources. The "wings" sometimes act like an "antidote" to counter our Core Type's tendencies. For example, Type One, being structured and rigid, can become more balanced and value relationships if this person has a strong Type Two wing. This gives rise to 18 variations (e.g. Type-Three-wing-Two and Type-Three-wing-Four, multiplied by nine Types).

Lines of Integration and Disintegration

The Enneagram model is dynamic yet systematic. The lines on the Enneagram symbol indicate the paths or directional moves a Type makes when that Type progresses (becomes more self-aware and developed) and regresses (becomes under stress and overwhelmed). Note that these are **metaphorical moves**, acting out the traits of the arrowed Type. It is not that one becomes and changes their personality into the arrowed Type. It is commonly believed that we do not change our Core Type.

- Line of Integration (figure 2.2)

  When healthy, each type moves towards the positive traits of another type. For example, Type One (Perfectionist) integrates to appear more like Type Seven (Enthusiast), becoming more flexible and spontaneous.

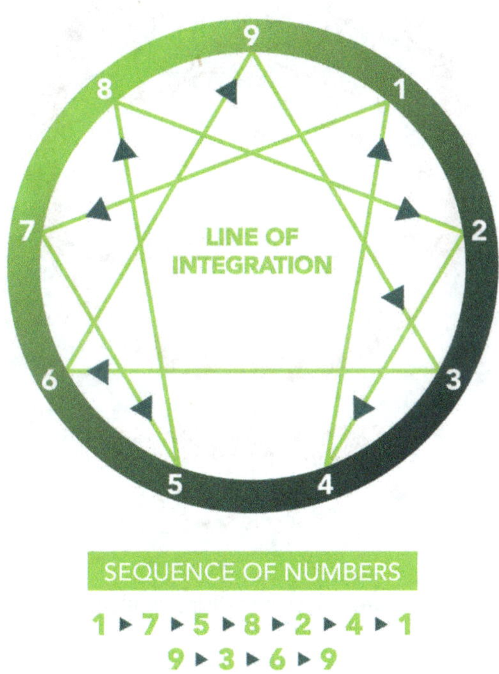

Figure 2.2: Line of Integration.

- Line of Disintegration (figure 2.3)
  Under stress, each type adopts the negative traits of another type. For example, Type One disintegrates to appear more like Type Four (Individualist), becoming more withdrawn and emotional.

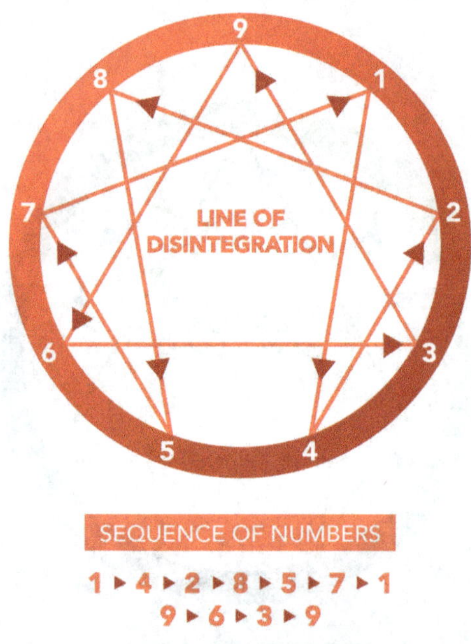

Figure 2.3: Line of Disintegration.

Some believe that there is only a single directional move as outlined by the arrows in the two diagrams while others believe that developments of each Type are bi-directional (i.e. each Type will show the negative traits of both arrowed types when under stress and show the positive traits of both arrowed types when developed).

Triads (Centres of Intelligence)

The Enneagram divides the nine types into three triads, each corresponding to a centre of intelligence: the **Head (Thinking)**, **Heart (Feeling)**, and **Gut (Instinctive)** centres. Each centre deals with core emotions and patterns:

- Gut/Instinctive Triad (Types Eight, Nine, One)
  Dominated by instinct and action, these types deal primarily with **anger** and issues of control.
  Type Eight: Expresses anger outwardly.
  Type Nine: Avoids or represses anger.
  Type One: Directs anger inward as resentment.
- Heart/Feeling Triad (Types Two, Three, Four)
  Dominated by emotion and self-image, these types grapple with **shame** and the need for validation.
  Type Two: Seeks worth through helping others.
  Type Three: Gains worth through achievements and success.
  Type Four: Searches for worth through individual identity and emotional depth
- Head/Thinking Triad (Types Five, Six, Seven)
  Dominated by fear and mental processing, these types are concerned with **anxiety** and how to feel safe.
  Type Five: Withdraws and seeks safety in knowledge.
  Type Six: Manages fear through loyalty or vigilance.
  Type Seven: Avoids fear by seeking pleasure and distraction.

Understanding these additional concepts deepens the complexity and accuracy of the Enneagram system. The interplay of instinctual subtypes, wings, lines, and triads creates unique personalities within each type, allowing individuals to better understand their motivations, behaviours, and areas for growth. When applied together with the utilisation presuppositions, these concepts offer a more complete framework for self-awareness and development, enhancing the transformative potential of the Enneagram. There are now many books, courses, and information about the Enneagram, we encourage practitioners to adopt a continuous learning mindset to hone their appreciation and understanding of the Enneagram to make the best use of this system.

TOP THREE SCORES IN PROFILES

There are a few presentation formats of Enneagram questionnaires in the market. Some profiles give you only the Core Type results and show you your "wings" and "lines of development" based on the Enneagram system. Other profiles give you the scores of all nine types, often presented in the form of a bar chart. In our Neuro-Linguistic Enneagram (NLE) profiling tool, we give you the top three types of your profile.

What does top three types mean in individual profiles? We believe that personalities are complex, and hence capturing the top three highest scores in a profile can be more accurate and comprehensive in the profile descriptions. A "high score" in the NLE profile merely means that your Core Type is likely to be in one of the top three types (often the type with the highest score; but not always), and you also embody many traits of the other two types. As such, a profile with "1-3-4" (Type One being the highest score; but not always, followed by Type Three and Type Four respectively) can be quite different from that of a "1-7-8" profile.

WHEN THE ENNEAGRAM IS APPLIED IN TEAM SETTINGS

The Enneagram is mostly applied to individuals and most of the literature and materials talk about personality traits. Since teams and groups are made up of people, I wondered if the knowledge can be applied to teams. My curiosity led me to a whole new world of Enneagram applications in team settings.

When applied in teams (I'll be using "groups" and "teams" interchangeably in this book to represent a group of more than one person, although "groups" and "teams" have different elements such as rules of engagement and purposes), the individual Enneagram profiles are aggregated to form a "team profile". The Enneagram profile can be interpreted slightly differently between that of an individual and that of a team (see table 1.1, overleaf).

Individual	Group/Team
There is a "Core Type" based on the high scores of the profile, usually the "highest score" but not always the case. Be it a "single high score/type" or "top three scores", the profile indicates "Types" or personality traits exhibited by the person.	There is a set of "high scores" when compiled, and because the profile is no longer of a person, each "Type" now becomes a "Dimension"—patterns shared and valued by a group of individuals. The profile indicates "tendencies" (in thinking, emotional, and behavioural aspects) when the group of individuals comes together.
A low score in a person's profile may indicate an area of under-development, which signifies inaccessibility or unused resources. In an individual NLE profile, we do not show the lower scores beyond the top three types.	A low score in a team's profile may indicate a blind spot or a minority group of people. Note that a low score in a team profile is still a dominant type for those individuals, thus it would surface as an "interactive neglect" if not addressed.

Table 1.1: The Enneagram Scores as Interpreted for Individuals and for Teams.

As such, in Enneagram team profiles, the interpretation focus will move away from individual Types toward interactive dimensions (or interaction dynamics). The motivation of an individual's Enneagram will still be there, but there is now an additional layer of social influence.

What does top three types mean in team profiles? A team profile of "1-3-4" will now mean that most team members have a Type One in their top three scores, followed by Type Three and Type Four in the top three scores given the personality make-up of this group. A zero score of any type means that nobody in the group has that Type in their top three scores.

Different Enneagram Types respond differently to social dynamics. For example, average Type Ones tend to be more controlled and moderated in teams, especially if there is a clear set of etiquette, structure, and rules to follow. Average Type Fives and Eights are more internally referenced and may not succumb or be affected by peer pressure in the group, still more dependent on their interest or impact focus. Average Type Twos would be more easily affected by the group members depending on the relationships.

Another way of looking at interaction dynamics is to imagine a room full of Type Nines, what would you think you might observe? Certain tendencies of Nines (such as moving around the room quietly and making friendly interactions) will show up more compared to a room full of Type Threes. When we look at team profiles, we can take on this lens to interpret the dynamics.

Chapter 3

NLE MODEL OVERVIEW

NLE TEAM MODEL

The Neuro-Linguistic Enneagram (NLE) Team Model is built on two established bodies of work: Neuro-Linguistic Programming (NLP) and the Enneagram. This unique fusion of methodologies has revolutionised the way we work with our clients, especially in building team understanding and optimising team dynamics to deepen trust and drive performance.

Drawing from the foundational principles of NLP, the NLE Team Model harnesses the power of language, communication, and neurological patterns, offering a profound understanding of the intricacies of human behaviour and the underlying drivers of individual and collective dynamics. Through NLP, the NLE Team Model provides the architecture, practical tools, and actionables that enable teams to enhance communication, cultivate psychological safety, and achieve alignment toward common goals, fostering team effectiveness.

Simultaneously, the integration of the Enneagram within the NLE Team Model adds a layer of depth and richness, offering profound insights into the diverse personalities, motivations, and behavioural patterns that shape team interactions. By leveraging the Enneagram's nine distinct personality types and their interconnected dynamics, the NLE Team Model enables teams to delve into the depths of self-awareness, empathy, and interpersonal understanding, thereby fostering a more aligned and cohesive team environment.

In the contemporary landscape of team dynamics and organisational performance, the NLE Team Model uncovers the essence of a team that transcends the boundaries of traditional team methodologies. At its core, the NLE Team Model is made up of the Team Map (a radar graph) and the Four Pivotal Points (4PP) Spectrums (see figure 3.1), which collectively redefine the understanding of team dynamics and to some extent, highlight predictive hypotheses about a team's conscious and unconscious tendencies.

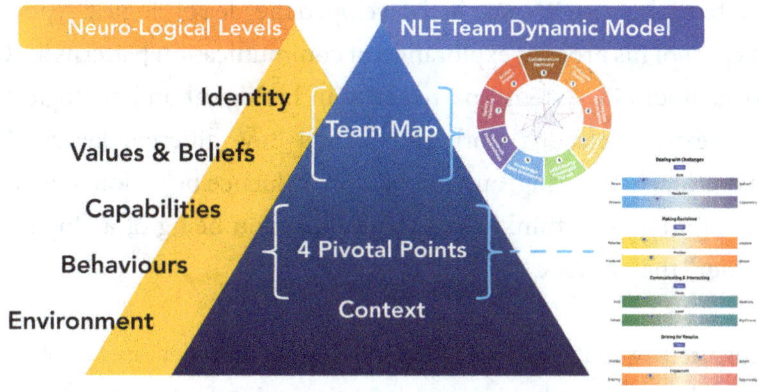

Figure 3.1: The NLE Team Model.

In any entity—be it a person, a team, or an organisation—there are neurological levels (see the yellow pyramid in figure 3.1) that define the congruence of that entity. In a person, this stems from how the person perceives him/herself (identity), the set of values and beliefs he/she has, and what capabilities this person has acquired, thus resulting in how this person behaves or acts in a certain way.

The concept of Neurological Levels in NLP was introduced by Robert Dilts, a key figure in the field, during the early 1980s. Dilts sought to create a model that explained different levels of human experience and how change could occur more effectively by addressing these levels.[10,11] He expanded upon the earlier work of Gregory Bateson, a respected anthropologist, social scientist, and

10 Dilts, Robert. *Changing Belief Systems with NLP*. Capitola, CA: Meta Publications, 1990.

11 Dilts, Robert. *From Coach to Awakener.* Capitola, CA: Meta Publications, 2003.

systems theorist. Bateson had developed the idea of "logical types" as part of his broader exploration of communication patterns and behaviours in systems, particularly in biological and ecological contexts.[12] Bateson's work emphasised how different layers of experience, thinking, and interaction influence behaviours, with certain types of thinking or communication being of a "higher order" than others.

Inspired by Bateson's insights, Dilts took this idea and applied it to human psychology and behaviour, developing a practical framework to help people understand and navigate the different layers of their personal and professional lives. This became the foundation for his Neurological Levels model, which organises human experience into distinct levels—ranging from environment and behaviours to deeper aspects like beliefs, identity, and even purpose or spirituality. Each of these levels represents a different layer at which change can happen, with the idea being those changes at higher levels (e.g., beliefs or identity) tend to produce more profound and lasting transformations, while changes at lower levels (e.g. environment or behaviour) are typically more surface-level and context-specific. This model became a key tool in NLP for understanding how individuals structure their thinking and behaviour, and how practitioners can guide people through meaningful, multilevel changes.

If any of these levels contradict one another or the person experiences inner tension (e.g. values perfection but the current ability indicates a lack of time to complete to a required

12 Bateson, Gregory. *Steps to an Ecology Mind: Collected Essays in Anthropology, Psychiatry, Evolution, and Epistemology*. San Francisco, CA: Chandler Pub, 1972.

standard), this person will become incongruent, get emotionally triggered, or get into a stressed state. Alternatively, it might also trigger the person to seek help and motivate this person to try something new. How this person would respond is determined by the "psychological health" of a person, i.e. how self-aware and self-mastered he/she is. We will explain more about a team's "psychological health" later.

Similarly, in a team setting, if the team identity and culture are pegged in a certain way, the team will likely adopt certain principles or values, and uphold certain ways of working, and the team members will carry themselves in a certain manner. Common examples of congruent teams are military groups, special forces, and certain government sectors.

Now, let's take a look at the blue pyramid in figure 3.1—Team Map, 4PP Spectrum, and Context—the Enneagram portion of the NLE Team Model.

TEAM MAP

In the NLE personality profiling, the top three types of an individual's Enneagram profile (out of the nine types) are identified. This approach allows for a more nuanced and comprehensive understanding of the individual, acknowledging the intricate blend of traits that shape their unique personality. The Team Map is formed when we aggregate every team member's profile and shift the focus from personality traits to team tendencies.

The Team Map (figure 3.2) serves as an illustrative radar graph of the team, portraying the composite of the top three scores from each team member's NLE profile. It offers insights into both the tangible and intangible dynamics within the team. Tangible aspects encompass behavioural patterns, communication styles, conflict resolution approaches, and other observable interactions. Intangible facets delve into the team's values, motivators, stress triggers, focal points of attention, and blind spots, painting a comprehensive picture of the team's collective tendencies.

Figure 3.2: Team Map.

The Team Map in figure. 3.2 has a profile of 1-5-3, i.e. most team members have Type One in their top three scores, followed by

Type Five and Type Three profiles. Consider a scenario where 30 individuals of the Type One personality are collaborating in a room. Reflect on what their collective values, motivations, capabilities, and behaviours might be. Do the same visualisation for a room of Type Fives and Type Threes (albeit fewer people in these types compared to the Type Ones in the room). By extrapolating this visualisation to a group skewed toward their top three scores, one can capture the unique "flavour" of the team's possible tendencies and characteristics. If you are familiar with Enneagram, it would be relatively easy to identify certain traits of this group—values excellence and quality standards, very task-oriented, likely to be detailed on plans and timelines, good in problem-solving, may neglect personal warmth, and can go into overdrive.

It is essential to note that the Team Map primarily reflects the team's tendencies rather than their competencies, which can be shaped by various external factors such as organisational systems, processes, and training. However, as Peter Drucker, a renowned management consultant, famously stated, "Culture eats strategy for breakfast", emphasising the profound influence of team dynamics on overall team performance and organisational success. If there are no conscious efforts to establish a team culture, this team dynamic is likely to take effect as the default.

In the NLE Team profiling system, each Team Map can accommodate up to four sets of data, which can be made up of a combination of individual NLE profiles and aggregated NLE team profiles. Consequently, the Team Maps facilitate various comparisons, including:

- Individual versus Individual (up to four individuals);
- Individual versus Team (up to a combination of four data sets); and
- Team versus Team (up to four teams).

The following examples illustrate a sample of three distinct Team Maps:

- Figure 3.3 presents a single data set of a team;
- Figure 3.4 showcases a comparison between the data sets of a leader (individual) and a team; and
- Figure 3.5 displays data sets from two different teams or departments.

Figure 3.3: Team Map of One Data Set of a Team.

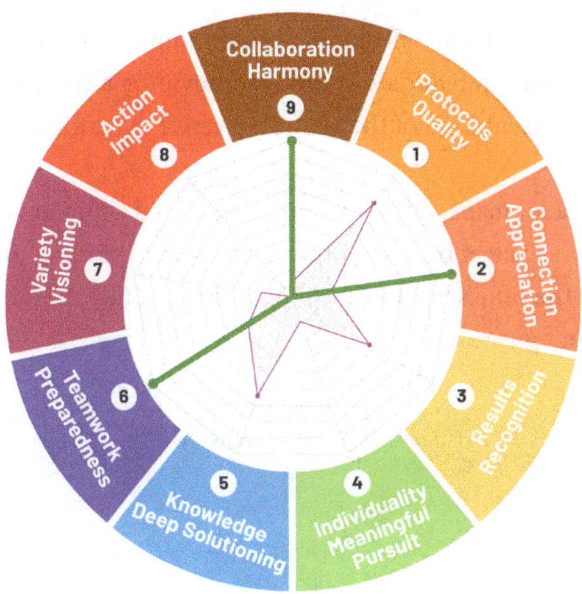

Figure 3.4: Team Map of Two Data Sets, Between Individual and Team.

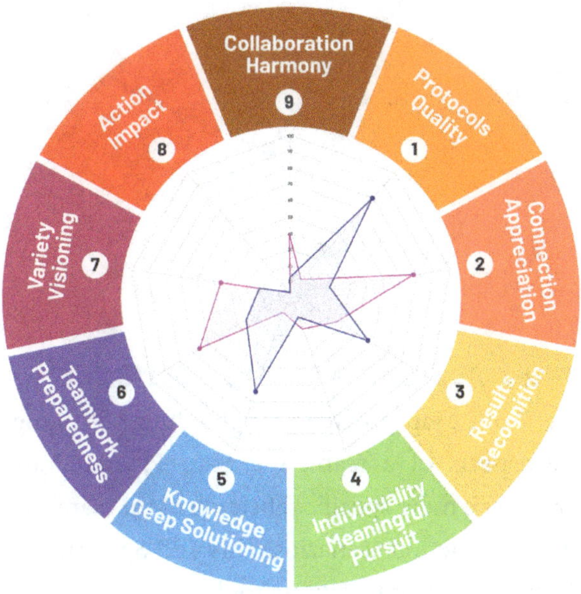

Figure 3.5: Team Map of Two Data Sets of Two Different Teams.

Each Team Map can effectively represent up to four sets of data, whether from individuals or groups, providing a comprehensive visual representation of the team's collective dynamics.

Similar radar maps can also be easily generated with the Microsoft Excel spreadsheet by using other Enneagram profiling tools that provide the nine scores in each individual profile. An example is shown in figure 3.6.

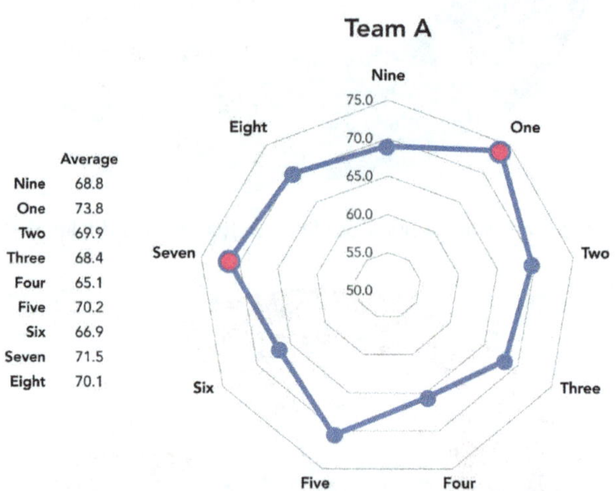

Figure 3.6: Excel Radar Graph.

FOUR PIVOTAL POINTS (4PP) SPECTRUMS

While the Team Map provides insights into both tangible and intangible aspects of a team, the Four Pivotal Points (4PP) Spectrums offer a more specific reflection of the team's tendencies in key team interaction scenarios. This 4PP Spectrums profile is unique to the NLE Team profiling tool.

Through our extensive consulting experience, we have noted that most teams primarily engage in the following four activities (see figure 3.7):

- Dealing with Challenges (problem-solving);
- Making Decisions;
- Communicating and Interacting; and
- Driving for Results.

Figure 3.7: The 4PP Diagrams.

In NLP, there is a set of mental frames known as Meta Programmes, which are cognitive styles of processing information. Given that these four touchpoints are cognitive by nature, we leverage on Meta Programmes, resulting in the 4PP Spectrums.

Why do we refer to them as "pivotal points"? Our consulting engagements have allowed us to observe numerous team meetings, recognising that each of these areas can serve as either a stumbling block or an area of potential improvement for the team.

Stumbling blocks, or choke points, manifest as challenges that hinder the team's progress. For instance, we've observed teams struggling to align on priorities, resulting in fragmented efforts and diminished overall performance. Similarly, teams overly reliant on linear decision-making processes might overlook the need for alternative approaches, inadvertently allowing decisions to be made themselves. Other stumbling blocks include teams operating within cliques and silos, leading to a lack of trust that undermines results. Additionally, some teams become so consumed with effort that they lose sight of the strategic intents, ultimately failing to generate meaningful business impact. Unaddressed, these choke points can impede team progress and lead to underperformance.

Conversely, these challenges present intervention opportunities. When teams recognise their inclinations and blind spots, they can implement systems, processes, rituals, rules of engagement, and protocols to counteract these tendencies. For instance, some teams establish structured meeting frameworks to identify problem statements and align priorities, while others create platforms for structured brainstorming sessions preceding critical decision-making. Certain teams invest in training every member on conversational structures, active listening, and effective questioning techniques to ease communication style differences. Other teams clarify roles and responsibilities to establish clearer accountabilities and foster improved performance.

Thus, these four areas can serve as both stumbling blocks and leverage points, earning them the moniker "pivotal points" as they possess the potential to pivot the team toward either beneficial or detrimental outcomes. Each pivotal point encompasses two spectrums, resulting in a total of eight spectrums. The positioning on these spectrums does not inherently denote "good" or "bad"—rather, it depends on the team's response to the demands of the situation. The positions on the spectrum merely highlight the team's tendencies and preferences; if the situation aligns with these inclinations, the team can manage it effortlessly. Conversely, when the situation contradicts their natural inclinations, it necessitates additional effort and intentionality on the team's part.

Positions in the middle of the spectrums do not necessarily imply "balance"; they may indicate either a team composed of two polarised groups or a team with the flexibility to navigate both spectrums. Conversely, it may also suggest that the team is grappling with indecision and stagnation.

Let us delve deeper into each of these pivotal points to gain a comprehensive understanding of their contributions to team dynamics.

Dealing with Challenges

Teams often coalesce to resolve challenges, accomplish tasks, and address issues. To achieve this, teams must establish a consensus on priorities, discern between problems and paradoxes, and determine effective solutions.

Regardless of the nature of the challenges, the team's approach reflects its inherent tendencies. Within this pivotal point, we examine two spectrums: Style and Resolution (see figure 3.8, overleaf).

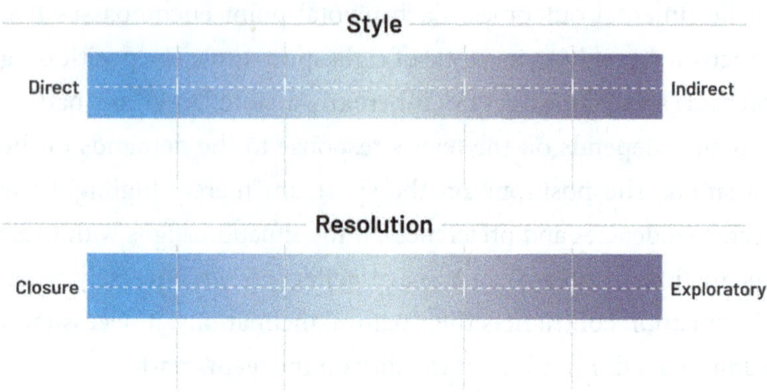

Figure 3.8: Dealing with Challenges—Style and Resolution Spectrums.

The Style spectrum delineates the team's preferred problem-solving approach as either "Direct" or "Indirect". A team inclined towards a "Direct" problem-solving style promptly addresses issues head-on, striving to tackle problems at their root cause and confront matters directly. Conversely, a team favouring an "Indirect" problem-solving approach may take more time to observe and allow certain issues to naturally resolve themselves, particularly when they are merely symptomatic or of a trivial nature. Additionally, teams with an "Indirect" style may exercise patience, allowing space and time for emotional sentiments to settle before intervening.

Style Spectrum

Direct	**tackling issues head-on, confronting problems, etc.**
Indirect	**allowing issues to evolve, tackle problems from the side, etc.**

The Resolution spectrum reflects the team's sense of urgency. Teams inclined towards "Closure" exhibit a strong commitment to resolving matters swiftly, demonstrating a robust follow-through in their actions. On the other hand, teams exhibiting an "Exploratory" resolution tendency possess the patience and adaptability to await further clarity, which proves instrumental in addressing complex and ambiguous challenges that demand a nuanced approach and comprehensive understanding.

Resolution Spectrum	
Closure	**a strong sense of urgency, resolving issues quickly, etc.**
Exploratory	**working around issues, keeping things open, etc.**

Imagine there are two distinct groups within a tech company navigating the ever-changing landscape of project management. Please meet **Team Catalyst** and **Team Voyager**.

Team Catalyst (on the "Direct-Closure" spectrums) is renowned for its Direct problem-solving approach and a strong penchant for Closure. The team thrives on efficiency and effectiveness. They are like the pit crew in a high-speed race, swiftly addressing challenges head-on and making rapid decisions. Led by a decisive leader who encourages a culture of immediate action and clear resolutions, this dynamic style has propelled Team Catalyst to success in various projects, earning them a reputation for quick problem-solving.

However, this unwavering focus on Closure comes with its own set of challenges. In their zeal to reach conclusions rapidly, the team occasionally jumps to decisions without fully exploring the nuances. This sometimes results in oversights and compromises the psychological safety of team members, who may feel rushed or unheard. The need for speed, while beneficial in many aspects, occasionally leads to a lack of thorough exploration, leaving some team members feeling their concerns are not adequately considered, hence undermining trust and commitment.

On the other side of the office, Team Voyager (on the "Indirect-Exploratory" spectrums) operates with an Indirect problem-solving style and a preference for an Exploratory resolution. They approach challenges like seasoned navigators, carefully observing the waters before charting a course. This team excels in managing workplace paradoxes and thrives in the complex, ambiguous environments characteristic of the modern workplace.

The Voyager team's strength lies in its ability to see the bigger picture, embracing the complexities of the VUCA world. The team leader encourages her team to explore different perspectives and take the time needed for a comprehensive understanding of each situation. This approach fosters a workplace where ideas are thoroughly examined, and the team excels at handling intricate, sensitive challenges that require nuanced solutions.

Yet, this penchant for exploration has its drawbacks. The team's comfort in ambiguity can sometimes lead to procrastination and a lack of follow-through. While they navigate the complexities masterfully, they might leave many things unresolved or postpone decisions for too long. This can create frustration among team members who seek immediate closure, potentially impacting project timelines.

In the office ecosystem, Team Catalyst and Team Voyager represent two sides of the same coin, showcasing the delicate balance between swift action and thoughtful consideration in the pursuit of workplace excellence. This pivotal point of "Dealing with Challenges" indicates a team's tendencies, regardless of their position on the Style and Resolution spectrums. The importance lies in being aware of what the situation or environment demands from the team and the ability to stretch beyond the tendency when needed.

Making Decisions

Decisions serve as the driving force behind actions, representing another pivotal reason for team performance. Within the realm of decision-making, several crucial components come into play:

- Decision Ownership
  "Who owns the decision?"—Identifying the accountable party or group responsible for the outcomes associated with the decision.
- Decision Definition
  "What is the decision to be made?"—Establishing a clear understanding of the precise nature of the decision at hand to avoid potential misunderstandings and confusion.
- Decision Process
  "How should the decision be made?"—Determining the appropriate method or approach to facilitate the decision-making process is often a point of contention within teams.

- Decision Timing
  "When should the decision be made?"—Pinpointing the optimal timing for making the decision, particularly when faced with unfamiliar or unprecedented choices.
- Decision Criteria
  "What criteria are we using to evaluate the options?"—Outlining the specific criteria employed to evaluate various options is a critical yet often overlooked aspect of effective decision-making.

Within this pivotal point, our focus centres on two fundamental spectrums: "Approach" and "Process" (see figure 3.9).

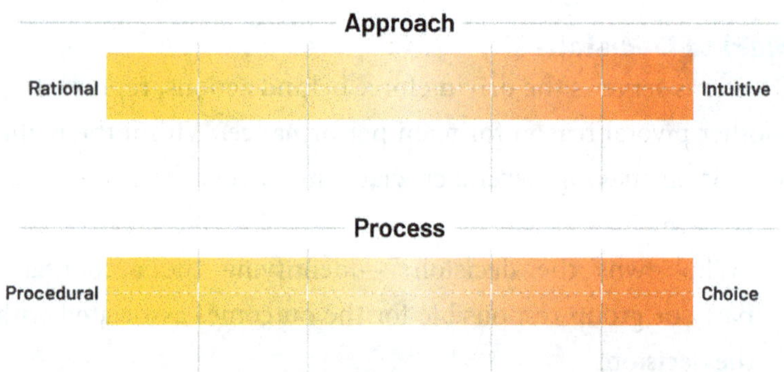

Figure 3.9: Making Decisions—Approach and Process Spectrums.

The Approach spectrum encompasses the evaluation approach of the team, characterised by either a "Rational" or an "Intuitive" decision-making style. "Rational" denotes a predilection for tangible data, logical reasoning, and analytical insights, while

"Intuitive" signifies a reliance on experiential knowledge, gut instincts, and intuitive perceptions.

Approach Spectrum

Rational	tangible data, logical reasoning, analytical insights, etc.
Intuitive	experiences, gut feelings, intuitive perceptions, etc.

The Process spectrum indicates the team's preferred decision-making approach. Teams positioned at the "Procedural" end of the spectrum favour a structured, often linear decision-making process that involves meticulous information gathering, comprehensive consultation, and methodical evaluation of options before concluding. Conversely, teams leaning towards the "Choice" preference exhibit a more flexible and less structured approach, often relying on a diverse array of options to swiftly facilitate decision-making based on a set of decision criteria.

Process Spectrum

Procedural	structured, linear decision-making processes.
Choice	agile, flexible, choice-based decision-making processes.

Let me introduce another two teams in the company—**Team Precision** and **Team Instinct**—who embody contrasting decision-making styles.

Team Precision (on the "Rational-Procedural" spectrums) is the epitome of systematic decision-making. They take pride in their rational and procedural approach, meticulously analysing data and evaluating options. Imagine a well-organised library, where every decision is catalogued, cross-referenced, and exhaustively reviewed. Their methodical leader ensures that the team's decisions are based on a thorough understanding of the situation so that getting buy-in from other stakeholders becomes a breeze.

This structured decision-making process consistently yields effective and well-thought-through outcomes. The team members are like architects, carefully crafting decisions with a solid foundation of information. However, this precision comes at a cost. The team occasionally finds itself caught in the web of analysis paralysis, struggling to make quick, timely decisions. The exhaustive evaluation can sometimes lead to missed opportunities, as the team is hesitant to commit without a full grasp of every detail. One case in point, they recently missed out on a great candidate in their recruitment effort because the hiring managers insisted on interviewing three more candidates for better comparison before they should conclude, even though this first candidate already met the hiring criteria.

Across the office, Team Instinct (on the "Intuitive-Choice" spectrums) operates with an intuitive and choice-oriented approach. Their decision-making room resembles a vibrant brainstorming session, where ideas flow freely, and options are explored with agility. The leader encourages a culture of adaptability, drawing upon the team's intuitive insights and a wealth of collective experiences.

Team Instinct thrives in a fast-paced environment, making decisions on-the-fly. They are like improvisational artists, responding to the rhythm of the moment. This speed, however, comes at the expense of clarity. The decision criteria might seem elusive, and team members may not always be clear on when a decision has been finalised. The dynamic, intuitive process might appear impulsive to those who seek a more structured approach, potentially missing out on influencing the outcome. Occasionally, decisions made have to be reopened and reconsidered due to a lack of proper engagement with key decision stakeholders or new incoming key information, resulting in numerous discussions.

In the bustling office environment, Team Precision and Team Instinct showcase the delicate dance between meticulous evaluation and spontaneous creativity. This pivotal point of "Making Decisions" illustrates the importance of finding the optimal balance to make informed, effective, yet timely decisions, depending on what the situation demands.

Communicating and Interacting

How team members interact and communicate with one another often serves as the initial lens through which we observe team dynamics, primarily due to its overt visibility. Within this pivotal point, we examine the two key spectrums: "Focus" and "Level" (see figure 3.10, overleaf).

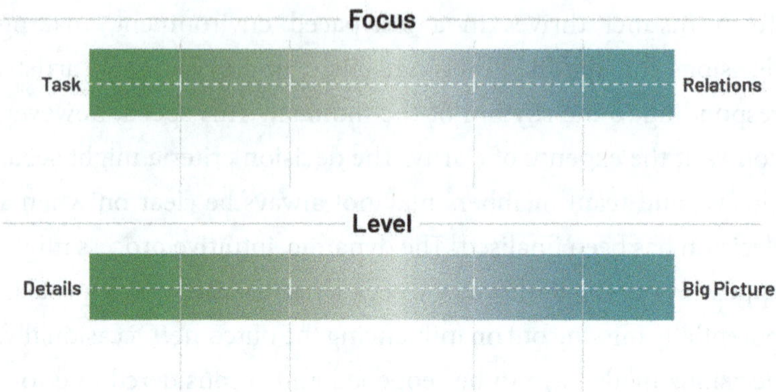

Figure 3.10: Communicating and Interacting—Focus and Level Spectrums.

The "Focus" spectrum is characterised by "Task" on the left and "Relations" on the right. "Focus" represents the primary area of emphasis during team interactions and communications. A "Task" focus team indicates a preference for discussing work-related tasks, exchanging information about actions and responsibilities, and emphasising practical aspects of the team's endeavours. On the other hand, a "Relations" focus signifies a more personalised and interpersonally oriented approach, fostering warmth, amiability, and customised communication tailored to individual preferences. This inclination towards relationships can manifest as a genuine interest in individuals, fostering a people-centric and politically adept communication style.

Focus Spectrum	
Task	task-oriented, work interactions, action-centric, formal, etc.
Relations	people-oriented, interpersonal, connection, informal, etc.

The "Level" spectrum spans from "Details" to "Big Picture," shedding light on the quantity and scope of information shared during interactions. "Details" implies a focus on intricate and comprehensive information, emphasising quantity, thoroughness, and precision in data exchange. Conversely, "Big Picture" denotes a preference for conceptual and abstract information, prioritising high-level strategic insights over granular details.

Level Spectrum	
Details	comprehensive, much information, thorough, precise, etc.
Big Picture	conceptual, high level, abstract, overview, etc.

Let's step into the vibrant headquarters of an AI-generated education institution where two teams, **Team Professional** and **Team Harmony**, personify the balance between task-oriented precision and relationship-centric collaboration.

In the sleek, modern office of Team Professional (on the "Task-Details" spectrums), every detail is meticulously curated. From strategic project plans to minute data analyses, the team values learning and sharing comprehensive information and updates so that everyone has what it takes to do their job.

Their no-nonsense, technically competent leader guides the team through intricate details, fostering a culture of in-depth understanding and technical mastery. Their meetings resemble boardroom sessions, filled with charts, graphs, and data points. The discussions are objective, focused, and incredibly thorough. However, the meticulous nature of their approach sometimes veers into a realm of cold objectivity. Team members are engrossed in data and may forget the human touch and emotional responses. Meetings, while productive, can feel long and draggy, bordering on disengagement.

On the other side of the office is Team Harmony (on the "Relations-Big Picture" spectrums) which operates in an environment of collaborative synergy. Their workspace is adorned with vision boards, fostering a culture of relationships and interconnectedness. They thrive on building strategic alliances, emphasising big-picture goals and overarching organisational objectives.

Their visionary leader encourages team members to empower themselves, handle issues independently, and contribute to the broader organisational narrative. Their meetings are more like lively discussions and debates, filled with stories and co-creative energy. However, the overarching vision can sometimes be so broad that interpretations diverge. Misalignment occurs as different team members envision the direction in varied ways. The emphasis on relations sometimes leads to a personality-driven culture, where individual perspectives may clash. In other situations, some subgroups prioritise the preservation of relations over results.

In this pivotal point, Communicating and Interacting, Team Professional and Team Harmony embody the best of both worlds—how to balance competent execution with inspiring storytelling. This equilibrium of balancing "Task" with "Relations" and bridging the realms of operational details and strategic alignment fosters open communication and builds trust, ownership, and commitment. It represents a coveted ideal for every company, aspiring to enable effective performance at every organisational level.

Driving for Results

Every team operates to achieve desired outcomes and deliver results. Within a corporate environment, this often translates to meeting specific financial targets, productivity metrics, or conversion rates. Within this pivotal point, we explore two essential spectrums that define how teams drive results: the "Energy" and "Engagement" spectrums (see figure 3.11).

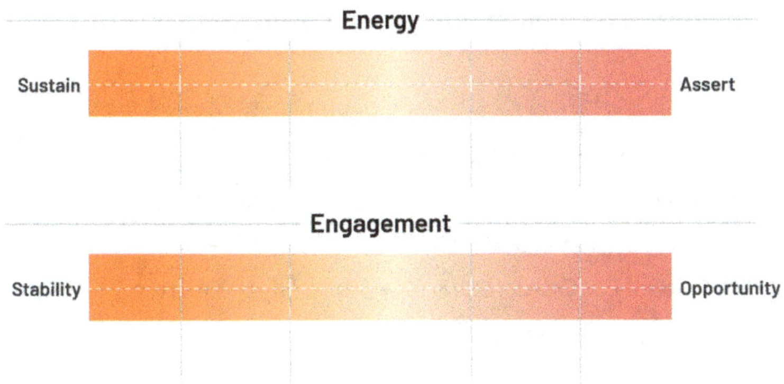

Figure 3.11: Driving for Results—Energy and Engagement Spectrums.

The "Energy" spectrum illuminates the team's approach to expending energy. At the "Sustain" end of the spectrum, teams tend to adopt a more conscientious and reserved approach, occasionally leaning towards passivity. Conversely, the "Assert" end of the spectrum signifies a proactive team that takes initiative and occasionally displays aggressiveness in pursuit of their goals.

Energy Spectrum

Sustain	conserving energy, more conscientious and reserved, etc.
Assert	taking initiative, proactive, more aggressive, etc.

On the other hand, the "Engagement" spectrum elucidates where the team directs its energy. "Stability" emphasises the importance of maintaining existing standards and operations, ensuring a focus on preserving current achievements and upholding the status quo. In contrast, "Opportunity" emphasises a dynamic approach, encouraging teams to explore new prospects, scale operations, and embrace innovative possibilities.

Engagement Spectrum

Stability	"do well", uphold the status quo, maintain the standard, etc.
Opportunity	"do more", try new possibilities, explore options, etc.

On another floor of the office building houses a few more teams: **Team Conservators, Team Enhancers**, and **Team Innovators.**

Team Conservators (on the "Sustain-Stability" spectrums) prides itself on anchoring the operations. They value stability, deepening their mastery, and upholding existing standards. The team leader believes in the mantra of "What is worth doing is worth doing well" and ensures that every task is executed with accuracy and consistently to preserve the team's reputation and credibility. However, the downside is apparent—the team tends to be overly passive, resistant to change, and sometimes settles for doing just the bare minimum to get by on areas not in their interests.

On the other side of the spectrum is Team Innovators (on the "Assert-Opportunity" spectrums). This dynamic group embraces an assertive stance coupled with a penchant for "Opportunity". They are the go-getters, always on the lookout for new possibilities and growth strategies. Their enthusiastic, optimistic leader ensures her team actively pursues innovation. However, there's a catch. In their pursuit of opportunity, the team may misuse their energy and resources and can become so engrossed in seeking new frontiers that their fundamental tasks and routines are not addressed, creating numerous self-inflicted crises that get in the way of their grand plans.

Team Enhancers (on the "Assert-Stability" spectrums) value continuous improvement, proactively building incremental changes to their operations, making things better, more productive, and more efficient. Their dedicated, responsible leader ensures that all their machines are well-oiled, and they pride themselves on being nurturing farmers of their trade, steadily and consistently producing results. However, because they tend to rely on past, proven methods, any new techniques and approaches are added on top of the existing foundations, leading to overwhelming and burnout.

This pivotal point of "Driving for Results" represents a different facet of how teams can perform and create results. In today's environment, challenges and problems come in different shapes and sizes, each demanding a different approach to handle. It is important for teams to find the appropriate way to drive the desired outcomes to balance growth and achievements.

In essence, both the Team Maps and 4PP Spectrums profiles serve as visual tools derived from the NLE profiling methodology. Team dynamics, often imperceptible, can pose significant challenges if teams remain unaware of their impact, leading to an uncertain performance trajectory reliant on chance or trial and error. Unveiling the team dynamics using the NLE Team Profile offers a promising pathway to unlock and harness the true potential of the team.

In the next two chapters, we will further unveil the insights of Team Maps and 4PP Spectrum in different levels of team health.

Chapter 4

DECIPHERING THE TEAM MAP IN 3R TEAM HEALTH

Team dynamics extend beyond the mere sum of individual personalities; they encompass a complex interplay of factors. Within this intricate tapestry, alignment occurs at three levels: intrapersonal (personal alignment), interpersonal (cohesion alignment), and environmental/purpose alignment (task alignment).

Intrapersonal or personal alignment pertains to the congruence of individuals within the team. This encompasses their level of self-awareness and self-mastery, delving into whether they exhibit resourceful states of mind or grapple with stress and feeling overwhelmed. As the adage goes, "We cannot not influence others"; hence, how team members present themselves affects one another.

Interpersonal or cohesion alignment refers to the level of trust and relationships within the team. Teams rich in trust and effective relationships demonstrate resilience in the face of tension and conflicts, even transforming these challenges into shared, constructive experiences that deepen the team's overall understanding and appreciation. Conversely, teams lacking trust and functioning transactionally may prioritise personal agendas for self-protection, intensifying strain on relationships within the team.

Environment or task alignment encompasses various aspects such as "why" (the purpose behind undertaking the task), "what" (defining the task and desired outcomes), "how" (strategies to accomplish the task), "when" (the timeline for delivery), and "who" (the team members involved). It refers to what the specific situation demands from the team. This alignment significantly influences the level of tension that the team must navigate, and if left unresolved, it can lead to interpersonal and intrapersonal misalignments, escalating tensions into personal conflicts.

Here are two examples to illustrate how these three types of alignment work together. Most teams are not so extreme; these examples merely aim to communicate the message.

- Team A comprises individuals who are low in self-awareness, and who tend to complain, blame, and justify when promises are broken. Other teams often find many of them difficult to work with. This contributes to a lack of trust and relations within the team and compounds the need to self-preserve one's interests. When the team is tasked to lead a change, the various cliques would squabble over fairness, resources, and management alliance.

- Team B is a high-performing team and comprises individuals who are mature and high in self-mastery. Dissatisfaction and conflicts are respectfully addressed and once decisions are made, alignment supersedes personal agreement. There is a deep level of trust and understanding among the team members, including their strengths and growth developments. Strong self and peer accountability are seen, coupled with strong support and collaboration to make things work. When the team is tasked to lead a change, every subgroup is driven by the team's common interest, and healthy negotiations and calibrations happen along the way to drive toward results.

In essence, "team dynamic" reflects the amalgamation of personal alignment (intrapersonal coherence), cohesion alignment (interpersonal harmony), and task alignment (environmental congruence), collectively shaping what we refer to as "Team Health". Although a standardised definition of team health remains elusive, drawing an analogy from personal well-being, we can define team health as the effective cultivation of conducive team dynamics that foster vitality and growth. Consequently, the alignment in these three dimensions assumes pivotal significance in nurturing and sustaining optimal team health.

Based on our extensive experience with diverse teams, we have observed three prevalent states of team health:

- Reactive Dynamic

  Teams exhibiting a Reactive Dynamic are often immersed in perpetual firefighting. In this state, individual patterns and fixations impede alignment, fostering a culture driven by self-preservation and personal agendas. Cohesion alignment deteriorates into the formation of isolated cliques and silos, marked by underlying political undercurrents and eroded trust. Consequently, task alignment suffers, leading to suboptimal performance, recurrent issues, and an overall survival mindset that overshadows collective objectives.
- Responsive Dynamic

  Teams embodying a Responsive Dynamic often demonstrate effectiveness, yet sustainability remains a concern. With a pronounced "we versus them" approach, these teams prioritise internal objectives, sometimes at the expense of broader organisational goals. While individual patterns contribute to the team's achievements, the long-term growth of team members might be neglected. Although cohesion alignment tends to be robust, it can become insular, potentially hindering holistic personal and organisational progress. Task alignment, though moderate, may prioritise short-term gains at the cost of sustained personal development and long-term organisational success.
- Regenerative Dynamic

  Teams operating within a Regenerative Dynamic epitomise sustainable excellence, akin to individuals embodying robust longevity. Such teams exhibit healthy collaboration and an expansive "we" perspective, incorporating organisational interests into their decision-making processes. Personal alignment is evident in the team's ownership, commitment, and the continual growth and development of individuals beyond their inherent patterns. Cohesion alignment, both within and beyond the team, fosters a culture of trust and inclusivity, enabling high-performance outcomes that resonate throughout the organisation. In such teams, leadership transcends mere hierarchy, representing a collective mindset and cultural ethos.

SAME TEAM MAP IN DIFFERENT TEAM HEALTH CONTEXTS

Within these varying states of team health, the manifestation and operation of the same Team Map can significantly differ. Consider the example of a 1-5-3 Team Map profile (figure 4.1) within distinct team health contexts.

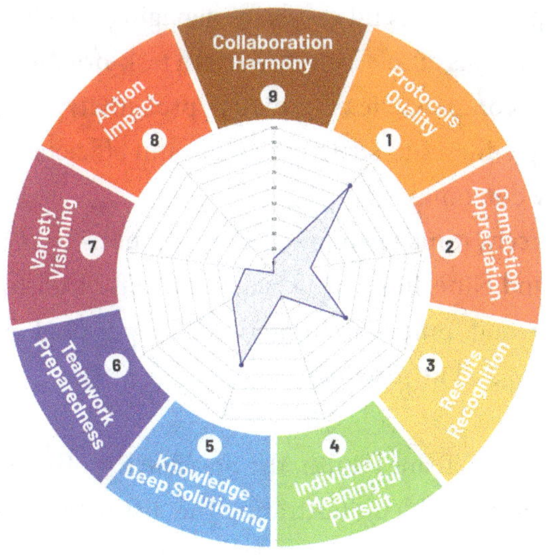

Figure 4.1: Team Map with 1-5-3 Profile.

Representing an operations team within a company, this Team Map reflects the aggregate of 30 team members' profiles, emphasising the top three scores in Types One, Five, and Three.

The general traits of this team profile are:

- Strong Type One dimension: Values high standards and quality, driven by processes, protocols, rules, and policies, methodical and organised in work approach, proactive in problem-solving with a strong focus on follow-through and closure.
- Strong Type Five dimension: Prioritises learning and deep problem-solving, guided by systems and problem statements, appreciates tangible criteria and data, and approaches tasks objectively and logically.
- Strong Type Three dimension: Emphasises results and outcomes, is driven by rewards and recognition, focuses on productivity and efficiency, is assertive in driving progress or solving problems, and excels in managing stakeholders.
- In essence, this profile leans towards a task-oriented approach, values competencies, exhibits proactivity in problem-solving, adheres to structure, logic, and efficiency, and seeks quality outcomes.
- Conversely, it may exhibit a lower emphasis on Types Eight, Four, and Nine, implying a lack of drive for transformational change and potential limitations in personal expression, diversity, and inclusivity.

For each state of Team Health, the possible hypotheses for Team Map 1-5-3 are provided, illustrating the distinctive dynamics in each context.

Team Map 1-5-3 in a Reactive Dynamic

- Overemphasis on problem-solving, driven by individual interests and agendas rather than team objectives, leads to constant firefighting.
- Siloed working and a focus on efforts over outcomes, resulting in fault-finding masquerading as problem-solving.
- High expectations for new members to be competent from day one, potentially leading to recruitment and retention challenges.
- Resistance and inflexibility, resulting in non-cooperation.
- Conflict avoidance, followed by problem-solving as the primary approach to conflict resolution.
- Transactional and impersonal relationships with a lack of care and concern.
- Limited collaboration as team members prematurely judge and reject each other's perspectives and ideas.
- The team dynamic is characterised by dominance by a few assertive members.

Jin's experience in this kind of office:

It was Jin's third week at this company, anxiety loomed as she grappled with an impending report due by Friday noon, and the elusive information needed to complete it. The office atmosphere was bustling with apparent busyness, yet a lack of assistance or concern from her colleagues added to her stress. Attempts to seek guidance were often met with silence, unhelpful responses like "I don't know", or impatient expressions.

Feeling a sense of urgency, Jin contemplated approaching another team head directly for the required information. However, she discovered a rift between this individual and her boss, leaving her uncertain about how to navigate the situation delicately.

The team culture emphasised written documentation for all correspondence with team members—especially with other teams—whether through text messages or emails, underlining the importance of self-protection. During her initial weeks, Jin felt the need to clear most emails with her boss to avoid missteps, resulting in lengthy email chains with multiple recipients "copied for information".

Participation in meetings proved to be a tedious affair, exemplified by an afternoon operations update meeting that was extended by an hour due to a team member's mistake, leading to visible frustration from her boss. The focus shifted towards scrutinising the chronological sequence of events and identifying opportunities to shift blame to another team to mitigate risk. This unexpected extension disrupted Jin's schedule for the next three hours, prompting an additional 30 minutes to rearrange subsequent meetings and discussions. By 6:00 p.m., Jin found herself exhausted, yet the day had yielded little tangible achievement. The demanding dynamics of the workplace were taking a toll on both her energy and productivity.

Team Map 1-5-3 in a Responsive Dynamic

- A focus on resolving team issues and challenges, prioritising the team's objectives.
- Cooperative behaviour, possibly accompanied by defensiveness in response to feedback; relying on an appraisal system and adhering to protocols or hierarchy for competency improvement.
- An inclination towards learning from past mistakes and failures, often in the form of case studies.
- Appropriate conflict resolution, with conflicts not actively encouraged; a lack of deep understanding among team members may persist.
- Cordial and relational relationships are subject to personalities; a level of trust is sufficient for task completion and friendly lunches.
- Defined niches of contribution, but personal growth and development may not be the primary concern.

- Generally good performance, though it may require managing tensions with other teams or stakeholders.
- A high-energy team with active participation and a focus on quality work within established parameters.

Wayne's experience in this kind of office:

Wayne successfully navigated his probation period, marked by a celebratory lunch courtesy of his boss, Dylan. Elated by this achievement, he reflected on the positive experiences and substantial learning opportunities during this phase. The team members, particularly Jolene and Fabian, proved to be generally helpful, contributing to his overall positive impression of the team. However, Wayne observed that a couple of individuals were less approachable, with Sam especially, standing out as the least accessible manager.

Wayne had a good experience with the whole onboarding journey. Buddies like Jolene and Fabian were assigned, provided him with the necessary guidance and information to him so that he could perform. Meetings were generally productive with the relevant parties contributing perspectives readily, but Wayne observed that most decisions would be made by Dylan.

Tasked with completing a report by Friday noon, Wayne hesitated to approach Sam for assistance. He noticed that the team usually left Sam alone, seeking his input only when absolute necessary. Wayne was aware that Sam could be cynical and sarcastic, occasionally bordering on aggressiveness, especially when busy—behaviours that seemed to be tolerated within the team. Moreover, Sam's recent promotion had stirred some discontent among team members, a sentiment Wayne picked up during casual conversations with his colleagues over lunch. A few of the colleagues began nudging a senior team member, Fiona, to raise the concern to Dylan. Fiona agreed to bring it up in her next one-to-one catch-up with Dylan, knowing his style of working.

After lunch, Wayne mustered the courage to approach Sam about the report, only to discover that Sam had taken leave that afternoon. While this provided temporary relief, Wayne acknowledged that he would need to address the matter the following day.

Towards the end of the day, Dylan expressed frustration—the Finance department had unexpectedly slashed the team's budget without prior consultation with him, leading to a sense of territorial and power encroachment. This revelation prompted Wayne to recognise the need to be more consultative within and across teams and be more cautious in future dealings with the Finance team. He also realised that maintaining close ties with his accountant friend might need to be approached more judiciously in light of the unfolding cross-departmental tensions.

Team Map 1-5-3 in a Regenerative Dynamic

- High-performing and capable of prioritising and readjusting based on changing circumstances and demands, effectively managing long-term objectives.
- A collaborative spirit, fostering the integration of diverse perspectives and ideas, leading to effective solutions and win-win outcomes.
- A culture of continuous improvement and robust feedback mechanisms promoting a learning environment.
- Early management of emotional dynamics to prevent personal conflicts, encouraging creative tension to foster innovative solutions.
- Relationships are founded on deep trust and personal understanding, with a strong emphasis on embracing diversity and respectful personal expression.
- Emphasis on individual growth and development, manifesting care and concern beyond formalities.
- Clearly defined roles and responsibilities, fostering accountability, strong commitment, and ownership.
- High-energy dynamics characterised by a robust can-do attitude, promoting extensive participation and engagement in team interactions.

Ava's experience in this kind of office:

Ava's last six months have been a fulfilling journey, marked by the successful completion of her probation. Although not without its challenges, as her boss engaged her in growth and development discussions from her first month, Ava overcame her initial uncertainties about her performance.

Her learning curve was steep, supported by a highly collaborative team that fostered a culture of accountability with clear roles and responsibilities. Meetings, while intense, proved to be impactful. Each team member provided a succinct report on their weekly focus, fostering self-accountability. When challenges arose, the team engaged in open discussions about their impact and implications, collectively contributing to solutioning. Ava marvelled at the co-creating spirit, witnessing the team building on each other's ideas to develop innovative approaches.

The team's camaraderie was evident, and Ava felt welcomed from day one. Each team member juggled dual focuses—the team's overarching objectives and personal development.

Fortnightly one-to-one check-ins became a platform for holistic discussions, encompassing everything relevant to these two focal points, often extending to individual care and concern and well-being amidst achieving the broader objectives.

Labelling this team as merely "winning" felt like an understatement. A new appreciation for the term dawned on Ava as she observed her boss, Jane, make a challenging decision to prioritise team resources for a synergy project with the Marketing division. This decision would impact the team's metrics, affecting Jane's KPIs and potential bonuses. Despite initial concerns raised by team members, the atmosphere was marked by open and challenging dialogue, showcasing a remarkable level of honesty and commitment. Jane, in responding to the tough questions from the team, displayed vulnerability and clarified the purpose behind the synergy project and what it meant to the company. It was a unique experience for Ava, witnessing tough decisions and conversations conducted with maturity, devoid of drama. The team's openness, authenticity, and unwavering commitment left Ava feeling blessed to be a part of this remarkable collective.

Through this exploration, it becomes apparent that team functionality corresponds to varying health levels. Team Maps and Team Health interdependently shape team performance, personal growth, and overall team culture.

In the following chapter, we will explore how the 4PP Spectrums profile manifests within distinct states of Team Health. Subsequently, in Chapters 8 to 12, we will provide practical illustrations of how team profiles (Team Maps and 4PP Spectrums) can be effectively applied in real-world scenarios.

Chapter 5

UNVEILING THE 4PP FRAMEWORK IN 3R TEAM HEALTH

The 4PP Spectrums comprise four groups of interaction points that emerge when a team comes together, reflecting the patterns observed in the Team Map. These interactions translate into tendencies that determine the focal points of a team. These focal points, or "focus of attention", significantly influence how a team tackles challenges, makes decisions, nurtures relationships, communicates, and drives results. Essentially, they offer insights into the underlying "team culture" that governs the team's functioning, ultimately contributing to team performance alongside its competencies and capabilities.

Team Map (Motivation)	+	4PP Spectrums (Focus)	+	Competencies (Skills)	=	Team Performance (Results)

Having previously outlined the defining spectrums for each pivotal point in Chapter 3, we know that the 4PP Spectrums can give rise to numerous permutations. The purpose of this chapter is not to teach how to interpret different permutations, but to delve deeper into how these four pivotal points may manifest within varying states of Team Health, continuing with the identical Team Map profile 1-5-3 as presented in Chapter 4.

Figure 5.1 is the 4PP Spectrums profile of Team Map 1-5-3 (figure 4.1). For each pivotal point, we will elucidate on how this set of tendencies might unfold within different states of Team Health.

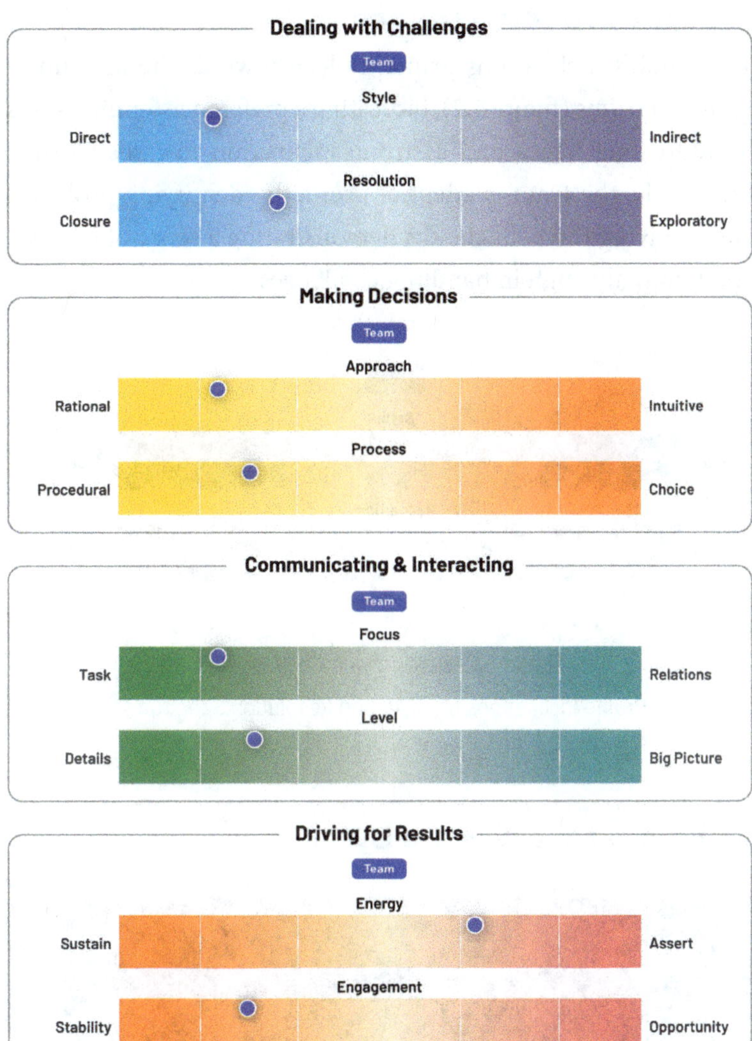

Figure 5.1: 4PP Spectrums of Team Map Profile 1-5-3.

DEALING WITH CHALLENGES

The profile's inclinations primarily lean towards the left end of both spectrums (figure 5.2), indicating a preference for directness in addressing issues and a strong inclination towards closure. Essentially, the team is adept at promptly identifying problems and resolving them efficiently, demonstrating a sense of urgency and follow-through in handling challenges.

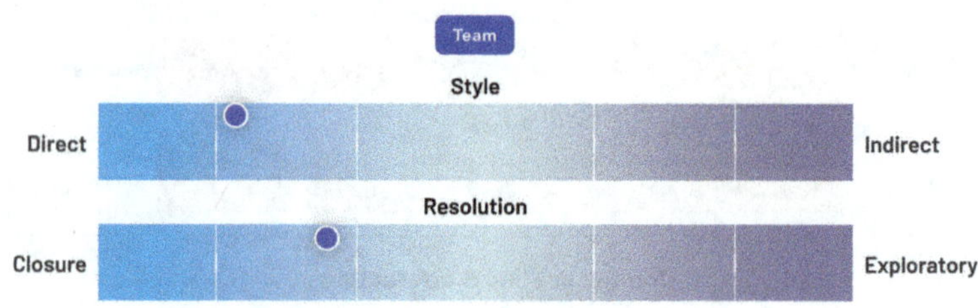

Figure 5.2: Dealing with Challenges—
Profile Inclinations on Style and Resolution Spectrums.

Profile 1-5-3 in a Reactive Dynamic

Recalling Jin's experience:

- The team quickly acknowledged the issue but when the problem became "unsolvable" due to an internal mistake, the priority shifted to blaming other teams to mitigate risk.
- The colleagues were not as helpful and overly task-oriented, causing Jin to feel isolated and unable to ask for help.

The team may tend to be overly critical and judgemental, sometimes mistaking bluntness for candour, leading to an environment where blame is readily assigned. This critical stance might inadvertently stifle the open exchange of ideas, prematurely shutting down perspectives without due consideration. In a team of 30 individuals, those less inclined to be direct may feel hesitant to raise concerns without proposed solutions, resulting in passivity and disengagement; hence, may use sarcasm or complaints to raise their concerns indirectly. Consequently, those more vocal about problems might shoulder an excessive workload, leading to a gradual decline in participation and engagement, perpetuating a cycle of constant firefighting.

The potential blind spots arising from a deviation away from the right end of both spectrums may involve a lack of patience in managing emotional tensions, overlooking the importance of allowing space and time for matters to unfold, and prioritising the pursuit of closing arguments over uncovering new priorities or truth.

Profile 1-5-3 in a Responsive Dynamic

Recalling Wayne's experience:

- There was tension among the team members but was neglected and tolerated.
- Certain team members (e.g. Fiona) would have enough trust and permission to have open conversations with the boss but it was not part of the team culture.
- While the team was supportive in general, cross-team interactions could take a territorial stance.

The team demonstrates proficiency in addressing challenges with an appropriate sense of urgency, fostering an environment where most individuals feel safe expressing concerns and pre-emptively identifying issues before they escalate. There is a collective commitment to addressing problems as a cohesive unit, facilitated by clearly defined roles and responsibilities that contribute to the team's overall efficiency in managing challenges.

However, within this context, the team may inadvertently overlook certain types of issues, potentially neglecting emotional tensions until they escalate into severe obstacles and treating them as problems to be solved rather than conflicts requiring careful emotional navigation. The team may also struggle with ambiguous and ill-defined issues, often setting them aside due to difficulties in comprehending the underlying complexities, thereby hindering effective collaboration with other teams and inhibiting the ability to navigate paradoxes.

Profile 1-5-3 in a Regenerative Dynamic

Recalling Ava's experience:

- Strong sense of urgency supported by self-accountability and solutioning to resolve issues.
- Team culture was open and authentic; team members felt comfortable raising their concerns and challenging the leader as part of the process to drive alignment and commitment.
- Jane's decision to prioritise the cross-team objectives above her team's and personal benefits.

Teams operating at this level possess a broader perspective, considering not only internal team challenges but also the implications for other teams and the larger organisational context. This expansive viewpoint enables the team to prioritise effectively, aiming for mutually beneficial outcomes that promote alignment, collaboration, and sustainable solutions. Despite the team's inherent inclination towards "Closure", they display patience in addressing certain challenges, allowing time for information to accrue, issues to mature, and clarity to surface. This patience is intentional and extends to the effective management of interpersonal conflicts and emotional tensions as people's sentiments are equally valid data points.

In a Regenerative Dynamic, teams display an increased capacity for flexibility and adaptation, constantly manoeuvring along the spectrums to maintain a dynamic equilibrium. Within this pivotal point, the team adeptly discerns issues that are best handled through indirect approaches, keeping them open for further exploration, or leveraging the perspectives of team members favouring the right end of the spectrums to ensure a comprehensive assessment.

MAKING DECISIONS

Similar to the previous pivotal point, this profile exhibits a notable inclination toward the left end of both spectrums (figure 5.3, overleaf), emphasising a preference for rationality and procedural approaches. Essentially, the team relies on tangible data and logical reasoning to inform decisions, adhering to a structured, linear process to arrive at conclusive outcomes.

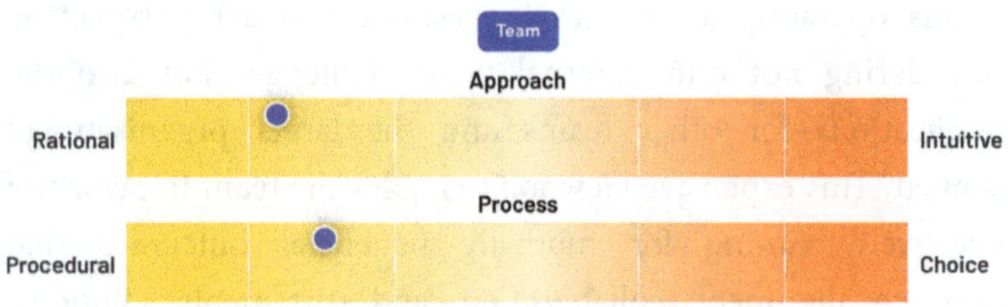

Figure 5.3: Making Decisions—
Profile Inclinations on Approach and Process Spectrums.

Profile 1-5-3 in a Reactive Dynamic

Recalling Jin's experience:

- The team scouted through a chronological sequence of facts and events, hoping to use this data to support their decision to avoid blame.
- Instead of focusing on addressing the impact and implications of the mistake, her boss got defensive and manipulative.

The team tends to be risk-averse, prioritising caution to avoid blame for any decisions made. Consequently, even urgent decisions undergo linear, process-driven scrutiny, with individuals manipulating hard data to influence buy-in, often neglecting or downplaying the significance of emotional sentiments. This approach results in decision-making lacking ownership and follow-up actions. People are defensive in the face of feedback and may be hesitant to contribute ideas to optimise the team's decision-making process. Strong personalities dominate decision-making, irrespective of whether they are the rightful decision owners. In situations with insufficient data, the team may stagnate and remain indecisive.

The potential blind spots stemming from a deviation away from the right end of both spectrums include missed opportunities to leverage the wealth of experience or gut-feel within the team. The team may struggle to make timely or swift decisions, only committing to choices when sufficient information or data is available. In the absence of clear ownership and commitment, the leader often assumes the role of the sole decision-maker.

Profile 1-5-3 in a Responsive Dynamic

Recalling Wayne's experience:

- Most decisions were made by Dylan with input from relevant parties.
- There was an implied protocol on how things should be done and who should be consulted. The assertive stance of "my team-versus-others" was obvious.

The team excels in decision-making, achieving both quality and consistency due to the structured process facilitating active participation and alignment among team members. The inclusion of people's sentiments is tempered by objectivity, limiting the influence of subjective biases on the decision-making process.

Productive debates and discussions centre on the issues at hand, although concerns and blame may be directed outward at other teams. While decisions may still involve the leader, input from all team members contributes to the final choices.

The team may inadvertently downplay the significance of individuals with extensive experience and gut feeling, favouring outcomes driven by structured processes. Consequently, when faced with unusual or challenging decisions, the team might arrive at suboptimal results. Additionally, the team's reluctance to reconsider decisions, particularly when prompted by external forces, may foster rigidity and resistance to change.

Profile 1-5-3 in a Regenerative Dynamic

Recalling Ava's experience:

- Jane's consultative approach with her team demonstrated how important decisions could be made in this state of Team Health.
- Jane's decision to prioritise the synergy project also illustrated ecology and win-win mindsets.

Teams operating at this level make well-informed decisions with ecological impacts, incorporating input from stakeholders to drive high-quality outcomes. The decision-making process, while structured, offers greater flexibility, often encompassing external stakeholders beyond the immediate team. Sufficient time is allocated for data collection and option evaluation, with clear criteria guiding the decision-making process. Proactive efforts to seek out and curate various options enable the team to tackle complex decisions adeptly. Once decisions are made, the team remains aligned and committed, remaining open to reassessments should crucial data emerge. At this stage, the team acknowledges the necessity of iterative approaches for innovative and complex decisions, treating certain choices as hypotheses open to refinement.

In a Regenerative Dynamic, teams demonstrate a heightened capacity to navigate along the spectrums, continually recalibrating their approaches to achieve a dynamic equilibrium. Within this pivotal point, the team harnesses the experience and gut feel of individual members, with the leader actively empowering team members to participate in the decision-making process.

COMMUNICATING AND INTERACTING

The tendencies of this profile are similarly skewed towards the left end of both spectrums, emphasizing "Task" and "Details" (see figure 5.4, overleaf) This suggests a team preference for task-oriented and detail-centric communications and interactions, engaging in comprehensive information sharing focused on professional dealings.

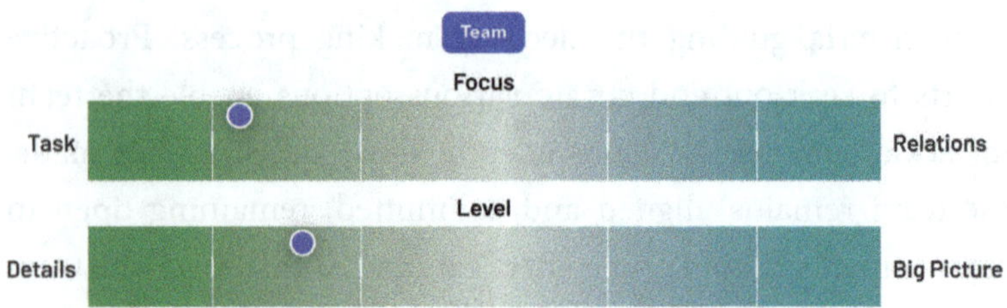

Figure 5.4: Communicating and Interacting—
Profile Inclinations on Focus and Level Spectrums.

Profile 1-5-3 in a Reactive Dynamic

Recalling Jin's experience:

- Everyone was operating in silos, resulting in a sense of isolation and lack of help for Jin.
- Prolonged meetings with a wrong focus led to inefficiency and self-inflicted firefighting.

Teams in this state tend to foster transactional relationships, engaging primarily on a "needs basis" without investing in deeper interpersonal connections. Communication often lacks a personal touch, with team members hesitant to dedicate additional time and effort to understand each other on a more profound level. Information sharing remains strictly confined to necessities, contributing to a culture of scorekeeping and selective disclosure, leading to communication breakdowns and a lack of trust. The team's meticulous approach leads to an abundance of unnecessary or unproductive activities, resulting in prolonged and inefficient meetings and discussions.

Common blind spots within the team include losing sight of the big picture and overarching objectives, disregarding the importance of people's sentiments and alignment, and struggling to motivate and secure the commitment of team members.

Profile 1-5-3 in a Responsive Dynamic

Recalling Wayne's experience:

- The team was generally supportive and friendly to Wayne, creating a positive experience for his onboarding.
- Wayne received sufficient information to do his job.
- On the surface, the team appeared cohesive, but there were undercurrents.

Teams in the Responsive state exhibit high levels of productivity and effective communication, conveying precise and comprehensive information with clarity. Professional and efficient interactions drive results, supported by a sufficient level of internal trust, leading to productive meetings and discussions. Regular updates contribute to a shared understanding, minimising misunderstandings and miscommunications.

While the team operates efficiently, it may overlook the necessity for fostering deeper interpersonal relationships, potentially undermining the development of a strong team identity built on camaraderie. Trust within the team might easily shatter during conflicts (hence conflicts are often frowned upon). The team's communication style could be excessively impersonal, limiting perspectives and failing to consider viewpoints external to the team, creating a potentially distorted perception of stability within the team while perceiving external teams as chaotic.

Profile 1-5-3 in a Regenerative Dynamic

Recalling Ava's experience:

- The team had open, deep conversations and felt safe to raise their concerns and challenge the leader.
- Alignment and commitment followed once decisions were made.

Teams operating at this level are influential and aligned with the broader organisational direction, fostering rich and holistic information exchanges both internally and externally. Well-organised information management systems (formal or informal) effectively disseminate information, enabling team members to perform their roles efficiently. Frequent feedback loops contribute to shared insights and learning across teams, driving diverse and conflicting agendas toward collaborative outcomes. While the team might not emphasise deeply empathetic and personal connections, it maintains a respectful, people-oriented, and supportive environment.

In a Regenerative Dynamic, teams demonstrate increased flexibility along the spectrums, continually recalibrating their approaches toward equilibrium. Within this pivotal point, the team is effective in addressing a wide range of communication and dialogues to foster ownership and alignment.

DRIVING FOR RESULTS

The tendencies of this profile lean more toward "Assert" and "Stability" (figure 5.5). This inclination signifies a proactive and high-energy team, focusing primarily on upholding stability and emphasising the quality of execution over the breadth of tasks completed.

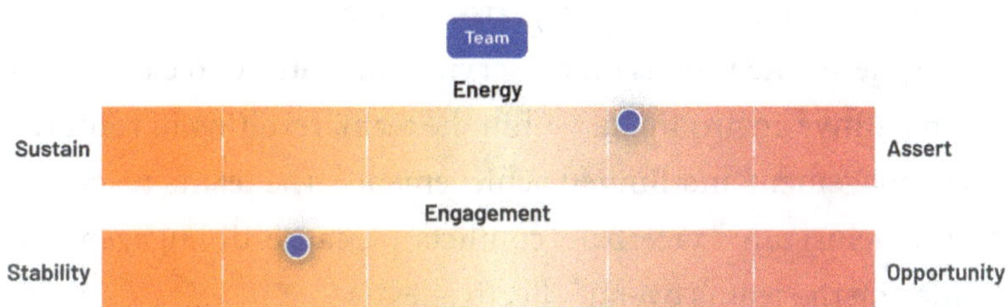

Figure 5.5: Driving for Results—
Profile Inclinations on Energy and Engagement Spectrums.

Profile 1-5-3 in a Reactive Dynamic

Recalling Jin's experience:

- Energy was spent on self-protection e.g. putting things in black-and-white.
- Mistakes were penalised with strong defensiveness, lacking accountability.
- Lack of cohesion and alignment by operating in silos.

Teams in this state often allocate their energy towards safeguarding personal agendas, fostering defensiveness and resistance to change, leading to an overly risk-averse and non-committal atmosphere. Their focus on preserving the status quo can lead to a competitive environment within the team, resulting in resource mismanagement and limited achievements. The team's reactivity to problems can exacerbate conflicts or cause disengagement, hindering the team's overall effectiveness.

Common blind spots include missing potential opportunities due to a lack of cohesion and alignment, hindering the team's ability to enhance performance. In this state, the team can become consumed by unnecessary conflicts and politics, diverting attention from their primary tasks and impeding overall performance.

Profile 1-5-3 in a Responsive Dynamic

Recalling Wayne's experience:

- Cross-team collaboration was clearly lacking, with an aggressive stance toward other teams.
- Some level of unhealthy comparison and competition existed as undercurrents, in this case, triggered by Sam's promotion.

Teams in this state are dedicated to continuous improvement, actively seeking feedback and implementing learnings to enhance their problem-solving capabilities. Task-oriented and focused on competency, the team conducts structured evaluations (e.g. post-mortem learning sessions) to drive incremental growth and improvement over time. Their consistent performance serves as a source of pride, fostering a winning mentality within the team.

The team might, however, neglect the importance of cross-team collaboration, remaining resistant to adjustments for the benefit of other teams. External requests may be perceived as burdensome unless they directly serve the team's interests, contributing to an ongoing tension and competitive dynamic against other teams.

Profile 1-5-3 in a Regenerative Dynamic

Recalling Ava's experience:

- The team embraced cross-team synergies, balancing long-term goals and short-term impact.
- There was a strong accountability culture that drove results and consistent performance, resulting in a winning team.

Teams operating in a Regenerative state actively support broader organisational transformation and growth initiatives. Their robust foundation cushions the impact of organisational changes, fostering a culture that embraces new methodologies and calculated risks. Creative tensions within the team are managed constructively, enabling effective resource allocation and progress tracking with clear accountabilities.

Teams in Regenerative Dynamic exhibit savviness in managing paradoxes, continually calibrating themselves to achieve equilibrium. At this pivotal point, the team learns to balance short-term and long-term goals, navigating the needs of the team and the organisation, and leveraging team members' strengths and development to foster growth alongside the business and the organisation.

INTERPLAY OF THE 4PP

The 4PP are closely interconnected and their effects on one another can significantly impact team dynamics. Different states of team health can intensify the challenges associated with this interplay.

While the team might identify priorities in one pivotal point, such as Dealing with Challenges, their communication patterns could potentially derail these intentions, resulting in unproductive discussions that hinder progress, keeping the team trapped in an unhealthy state. Conversely, in a healthy team (Responsive or Regenerative), interventions at any pivotal point can have a positive ripple effect, leading to overall enhancement and effectiveness.

Identifying the starting point for improvement will rely on in-depth on-site observations of the team, viewed through a consulting lens. Evaluating the interplay of the 4PP within any team profile will offer a clearer understanding of the existing dynamics and help strategise targeted interventions for optimal results.

Generally, in a Reactive Dynamic

In this particular state of health, team alignment is generally lacking, leading to busy yet unproductive individuals who fail to contribute to team or organisational objectives. Compounding this issue is the potentially domineering decision-making style of certain individuals (or the leader), while others remain passive and disengaged. Furthermore, the team's communication style may neglect or amplify underlying emotions, sentiments, and concerns, creating a mismatch between verbal and non-verbal cues or mixed signals. As a result, team members may become more focused on serving their personal agendas and interests, ultimately undermining the team's overall performance and effectiveness.

Addressing the challenges in this state of health requires a holistic and multifaceted approach, beginning with an evaluation of leadership quality and team members' competencies. Typically, we need to start with the leader and leverage on systems and processes. To rectify the issues within the 4PP Spectrums, the following strategies could be considered:

- Dealing with Challenges
  Foster alignment by establishing clear priorities and implementing cohesive strategies, action plans, and timelines. Designate key drivers and accountable individuals while considering the implementation of project management frameworks, if necessary.
- Making Decisions
  Identify critical decisions and clarify the corresponding decision owners responsibility for their outcomes. Align decision timing and criteria and facilitate the optimisation of available options.
- Communicating and Interacting
  Establish effective rules of engagement and provide communication skills training for all team members. Develop a common language to define terms such as "urgency" and "priority," and promote specific interaction etiquette (e.g. prompt communication regarding lateness for meetings, mandatory participation during meetings, etc.) to improve the quality of interactions.
- Driving for Results
  Clearly define roles and responsibilities to enhance accountability within the team. Hold decision owners responsible for unfulfilled commitments and celebrate and recognise achievements to encourage the pursuit of impactful outcomes. Regularly monitor progress and prioritise discussions centred on the consequences and implications of actions taken.

Generally, in a Responsive or Regenerative Dynamic

In these two states of health, the team typically exhibits strong alignment and good performance. Effective problem-solving is complemented by optimal decision-making, facilitated by clear and open communication and a healthy level of trust among team members. This environment fosters motivation and encourages active contributions toward team performance.

When the team is in a Responsive Dynamic, the priority is to broaden their perspective to include others in their considerations. On the other hand, when the team is in a Regenerative Dynamic, the focus shifts towards cultivating deeper learning and promoting team growth.

For any team in a Responsive Dynamic, the following strategies can be employed to expand their world view:

- Dealing with Challenges

  Establish connections between the team's objectives and the broader organisational goals, and shift the emphasis from "cost and benefits" to "impact and implications" of their actions on the organisation's success.
- Making Decisions

  Involve stakeholders from outside the team in the decision-making process, considering both short-term and long-term outcomes to balance the team's needs with those of the organisation.
- Communicating and Interacting

  Foster a culture of frequent information exchanges, both formally and informally, across teams. Encourage a feedback culture to promote open communication.

- Driving for Results
  Celebrate wins and successes, involving other teams that have contributed. Establish platforms for collaboration and co-creation and seek support from other teams for more complex initiatives.

In a Regenerative Dynamic, the focus shifts to deepening learning and fostering growth within the team. The following strategies can aid in achieving this objective:

- Dealing with Challenges
  Set challenging goals that push the team's boundaries and restructure the team to enable greater empowerment and agility in problem-solving.
- Making Decisions
  Provide training or simulations on making difficult decisions, eliciting the core values and principles. Delegate decision ownership to the next level, supported by mentorship.
- Communicating and Interacting
  Cultivate camaraderie through shared experiences, both real and simulated, to deepen personal understanding and empathy. Establish practices that celebrate accomplishments and provide frequent affirmations.
- Driving for Results
  Encourage self-accountability and develop a culture of peer accountability. Facilitate the formation of self-organised learning groups to enrich the team's growth and development.

Chapter 6

LEADERSHIP AND TEAM DYNAMICS

Leadership is a pivotal element in driving team performance and achieving organisational success. Traditionally seen as the responsibility of an individual leader, leadership in today's VUCA world is increasingly viewed as a shared effort of the team. Understanding both the team's and the leader's profiles is critical in creating a cohesive and productive team dynamic. This chapter delves into the impact and implications of effective leadership on team dynamics, and how an insightful comparison of profiles can help leaders be more targeted in developing the team as a whole (instead of just focusing on individuals' competencies), drawing on the insights gleaned from the aforementioned team profile information.

Today, a multidimensional approach to leadership is essential, encompassing the three levels of alignment—intrapersonal (personal), interpersonal (cohesion), and environmental (task)—as elaborated on in Chapter 4. In the last 20 years, various leadership concepts have emerged. Among my favourite books are Jim Collins's *Good to Great* which emphasises "Level 5 Leadership" that blends personal humility and professional will,[13] and Simon Sinek's *Start with Why* and *Leaders Eat Last* underscore the importance of purpose-driven leadership and fostering trust within teams.[14,15] Additionally, Patrick Lencioni's *The Five Dysfunctions of a Team* (and how to overcome them) offers practical strategies for addressing common barriers to collaboration, illustrating the balance required between interpersonal dynamics and task management.[16,17] Brené Brown's work in *Dare to Lead* further highlights the role of vulnerability and courageous conversations in building authentic and effective leadership.[18]

---

13 Collins, James. *Good to Great: Why Some Companies Make the Leap ... and Others Don't.* New York, NY: HarperCollins Publishers, 2001.

14 Sinek, Simon. *Start with Why: How Great Leaders Inspire Everyone to Take Action.* New York: Portfolio, 2009.

15 Sinek, Simon. *Leaders Eat Last: Why Some Teams Pull Together and Others Don't.* New York: Portfolio, 2014.

16 Lencioni, Patrick. *The Five Dysfunctions of a Team: A Leadership Fable*. San Francisco, CA: Jossey-Bass, 2002.

17 Lencioni, Patrick. *Overcoming the Five Dysfunctions of a Team: A Field Guide for Leaders, Managers, and Facilitators*. San Francisco, CA: Jossey-Bass, 2010.

18 Brown, Brené. *Dare to Lead: Brave Work. Tough Conversations. Whole Hearts*. New York, NY, Random House, 2018.

Leadership is complex. In my opinion, each of the above leadership concepts mentioned in the previous paragraph is not mutually exclusive, but more of illustrating the diverse facets and needs of leadership. This is why leadership is often a collective effort—the leader needs the team, both individuals and as a group dynamic, to make things happen and create desired results.

All these leadership styles, be they transformational, adaptive, or authentic leadership, cannot happen without the leaders having deep insights into their leadership patterns and tendencies, and that of the team dynamic. Tools like the NLE Team Profile provide leaders with a nuanced understanding of team dynamics, shedding light on hidden strengths and areas for improvement. By incorporating such evidence-based models and principles, leaders are better equipped to navigate complexities, promote trust, and align team objectives with organisational goals. This integrated perspective ensures not only effective task execution but also the long-term health and adaptability of teams in an ever-changing business landscape.

Here is an illustration of how a leader and team profile comparison can bring insights to the group, and help the leader identify and select pivotal interventions to enhance team understanding and alignment.

In this real scenario, the team has had some attrition and almost 40% of the staff are new. This "almost new" team exhibits a 1-5-3 profile, indicating a tendency toward a Responsive state of team health. Meanwhile, the leader possesses a 2-9-6 profile, characterised by a strong people-oriented approach, emphasising servant leadership, supportive and appreciative, with a nurturing style. However, potential drawbacks of this leadership style include subjectivity, avoidance of conflict to preserve relationships, emotional decision-making, and possible boundary issues.

A comprehensive comparison using the Team Map and 4PP Spectrums is detailed in figure 6.1.

Figure 6.1: Comprehensive Comparison—Leader (2-9-6) / Team (1-5-3).

TEAM MAPS COMPARISON: RESPONSIVE DYNAMIC

Both the leader and the team exhibit a strong sense of responsibility, cooperation, and commitment to achieving their objectives. The leader demonstrates a nurturing and empowering approach, showcasing a keen ability to identify and leverage team members' strengths and foster a cohesive work environment. Despite all the understaffing and staff turnover, she has successfully built positive relationships and earned the trust of the team, even with the newcomers, in a short span of time.

The leader is very engaging and nurturing especially to new hires, ensuring that they are well taken care of, get everything they need to learn and do their roles, and have frequent check-ins on their well-being. The leader generally encourages team empowerment and often seeks their input in decision-making, consistently showing appreciation for their contributions. While the team recognises her active listening and coaching, and motherly approach, they express a desire for more direct feedback, clearer instructions, and firmer decisions (instead of frequent reopening of decisions made).

The team values the leader's hands-off management approach, allowing them autonomy in problem-solving while the leader focuses on managing external stakeholders' expectations. They appreciate the network and good relations built by the leader with other teams in the organisation, as this often results in smooth operations and effective stakeholder management. Simultaneously, the leader acknowledges and values the team's competence and proactive approach to resolving challenges. She feels that she has the support of the team in return and looks forward to developing this team.

4PP SPECTRUMS COMPARISON: RESPONSIVE DYNAMIC

Dealing with Challenges

In this pivotal point (see figure 6.2), there is a noticeable disparity between the team's preferences, which lean towards direct and clear guidance, and the leader's inclination for a more nuanced approach. The team members desire the leader to provide explicit direction, establish clear priorities, and directly confront any existing issues. On the other hand, the leader may adopt a more cautious approach, considering the team's feelings and hesitating to make immediate conclusions. She might perceive certain issues as interconnected and complex, opting to address them indirectly or take more time to gather information, particularly because of her recent arrival at the organisation.

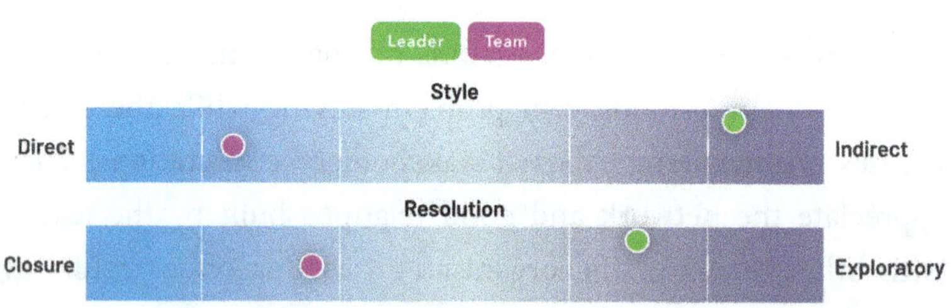

Figure 6.2: Dealing with Challenges—Leader (2-9-6) / Team (1-5-3).

If this discrepancy persists without a deeper understanding of the underlying dynamics, the team might interpret the leader's approach as overly subjective and ineffective, resulting in recurring issues and a diminished sense of urgency. Conversely, the leader might view the team as demanding, impatient, and reactive to challenges. However, as a collective, they can complement each other effectively, with the leader focusing on managing key stakeholders and the team handling routine operational matters. This arrangement can prove highly beneficial, especially if the team is adept at proactively resolving recurring issues, allowing the leader to concentrate on navigating complex, people-centric challenges and demands.

Making Decisions

In this pivotal point (see figure 6.3), the leader demonstrates a reliance on intuition and extensive experience, often looking to her instincts and perceptions of the situation to make decisions. She exhibits a willingness to make swift decisions when presented with favourable options but is also comfortable with leaving matters open-ended when more information is required, allowing time for understanding and emotional considerations. This approach has served her well in navigating complex corporate environments throughout her career.

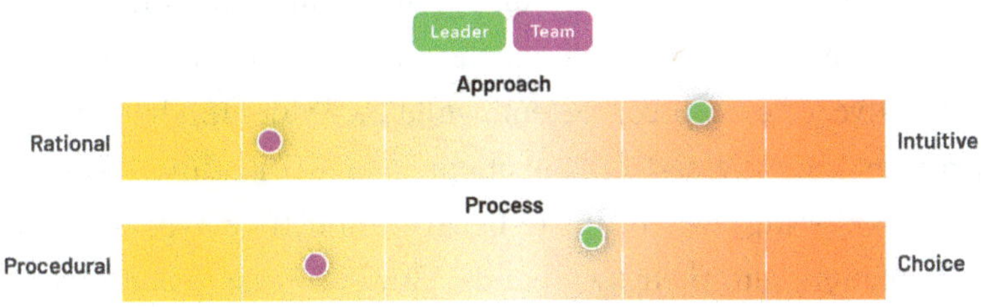

Figure 6.3: Making Decisions—Leader (2-9-6) / Team (1-5-3).

Conversely, the team members exhibit a preference for concrete data points and structured decision-making processes. They generally adhere to established procedures, which provide a clear framework for contributing opinions, following through with decisions, and executing tasks. This structured approach enables the team to swiftly resolve issues and transition seamlessly to the next challenge, as outlined in the earlier pivotal point.

Initially, the team may find the leader's decision-making process confusing, given her tendency to conclude swiftly on certain occasions while keeping decisions open-ended for others. This inconsistency, coupled with ongoing side conversations that influence decisions, may leave team members unsure about when to offer their perspectives and when the leader might reopen discussions. Considering her recent entry into the organisation, the team extends the benefit of the doubt, assuming that she may require additional information to reach decisions more efficiently. Consequently, they proactively provide information to aid in expediting the decision-making process.

If left unaddressed, this discrepancy in decision-making preferences may lead the team to perceive the leader as indecisive, subjective, or even incompetent, while the leader might view the team as overly assertive, impatient, and demanding, possibly even exhibiting insubordinate behaviours if they bypass her or take matters into their own hands. However, as a cohesive unit, they have the potential to complement each other effectively, with the leader contributing her extensive external experience and the team offering valuable technical expertise and a comprehensive understanding of the internal dynamics within the organisation.

Communicating and Interacting

In this pivotal point (see figure 6.4), the team and the leader exhibit a shared inclination toward detail-oriented approaches, facilitating comprehensive and in-depth exchanges of information. However, a notable distinction emerges between the team's preference for discussing task-oriented matters and the leader's heightened sensitivity to interpersonal dynamics. While the leader maintains a focus on tasks, her attention tends to be more attuned to relational aspects, exhibiting a keen awareness of subtle cues such as body language and emotional dynamics, rather than solely relying on technical data.

Figure 6.4: Communicating and Interacting—Leader (2-9-6) / Team (1-5-3).

Consequently, the team may perceive the leader as excessively friendly or intrusive, potentially questioning her technical competency in guiding day-to-day discussions effectively. In contrast, the leader might view the team as overly impersonal, potentially overlooking the importance of securing stakeholder buy-in and fostering commitment among team members. Should these perceptions persist without deeper mutual understanding, the team may ultimately question the leader's ability to contribute meaningfully or provide effective guidance, while the leader might perceive the team as overly technical and lacking broader political viewpoints.

Moreover, both the leader and the team risk losing sight of the larger organisational objectives, potentially resulting in a scenario where their busy schedules throughout the year fail to yield substantial strategic impact. It is essential for both parties to bridge this understanding gap and cultivate a more comprehensive perspective that encompasses both task-oriented efficiency and an appreciation for the human dynamics within the organisational framework. This holistic approach can enable them to align their efforts more effectively with the organisation's overarching goals and objectives.

Driving for Results

In this pivotal point (see figure 6.5), the alignment between the team and the leader is evident in their shared commitment to continuous improvement. The leader demonstrates proactive support for her team, emphasising the development of team members and the harnessing of individual strengths. Owing to her relational focus and preference for keeping certain aspects open, the leader motivates the team, leveraging the strengths of each member to drive results. However, her communication style, as highlighted in the third pivotal point, might hinder her ability to provide direct and honest developmental feedback, as she may fear jeopardising her relationships with team members.

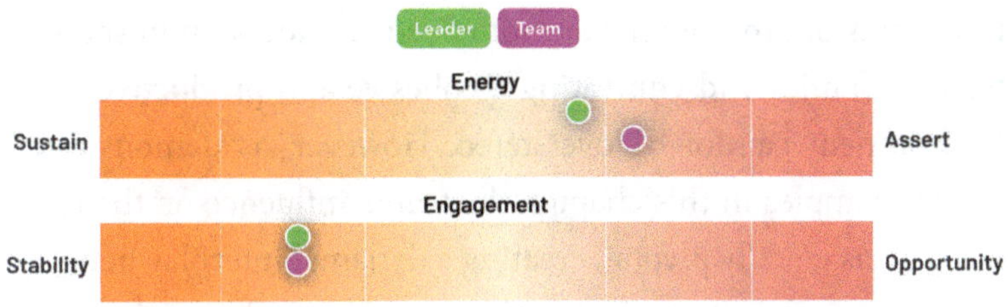

Figure 6.5: Driving for Results—Leader (2-9-6) / Team (1-5-3).

Given the parallels in their profiles at this juncture, a congruence is likely observed in the team's operational approach, particularly when the leader empowers the team and the team, in turn, demonstrates competence and structure in handling daily tasks. However, the leader may encounter challenges in establishing structured systems for methodically tracking progress and holding the team accountable for any unfulfilled commitments.

Both the team and the leader might encounter difficulties in navigating transformative growth or changes, given their inclination toward "doing well" rather than "doing more". This mindset could lead to missed opportunities for innovative and substantial changes, prompting resistance from both the team and the leader. The team may resist changes to preserve the reliability of established structures and processes, while the leader may resist due to concerns about potential disruptions to the team's well-being and morale or when the proposed changes do not align with the team's overall benefit. It is essential for the team and the leader to recognise the potential benefits of embracing change and innovation, thereby fostering an environment conducive to sustained growth and development.

In conclusion, the significance of effective leadership in shaping team dynamics and cultivating a cohesive and productive team environment cannot be overstated. However, as demonstrated in the examples in this chapter, the team's influence on the team dynamic is equally pivotal, creating a dynamic interplay between leadership and the team. This interactive relationship underscores the evolving nature of leadership in the contemporary VUCA environment, where the collective participation and contribution of every team member are vital.

Consequently, organisations are encouraged to reimagine their approach to leadership and team dynamics, shifting their focus from individual leadership development to embedding leadership within every team. This approach empowers the entire team to take ownership of optimising team dynamics and enhancing team effectiveness, fostering a culture of shared leadership and collaboration.

Chapter 7

TEAM NEURO-ACTIONABLES

Leaders often wonder, "What now?" after gaining insights into their own and their team's profiles. The question becomes how to apply this understanding to improve team dynamics and outcomes effectively.

Team neuro-actionables are targeted strategies and interventions rooted in neuroscience and NLP designed to enhance collaboration, communication, and team performance. By leveraging principles from neuroscience and NLP, leaders can create environments conducive to creativity, innovation, and problem-solving. These actions address cognitive, emotional, and social dynamics within a team. Examples include:

- Encouraging frequent feedback to build a culture of openness and trust;
- Incorporating team-building exercises to foster empathy and camaraderie;
- Providing resources for managing stress and emotional regulation to improve resilience;
- Ensuring psychological safety through inclusive practices that welcome diverse perspectives;
- Refining communication structures and linguistic distinctions to enhance clarity and mutual understanding;
- Supporting work-life balance with rituals and practices that promote well-being; and
- Facilitating collaborative tasks that leverage cognitive diversity to boost problem-solving.

Team performance is influenced by various internal and external factors, making organisational development (OD) interventions crucial for aligning structural, leadership, HR, and business strategies. In the NLE team dynamic model, tactical shifts and targeted interactions are central to improving team engagement. These neuro-actionables fall into three broad categories:

- Mindset

  Shaping the team's collective focus and attitudes toward shared goals and challenges.
- Dialogue

  Strengthening emotional connections through effective communication and nuanced language use.

- Actions
  Implementing tangible processes and platforms that streamline collaboration and enhance day-to-day interactions.

By integrating these elements, leaders can foster sustainable improvements in team dynamics, translating insights into actionable outcomes that drive performance and success. Often, they are also part of OD consulting recommendations and scope.

The tables that follow (tables 7.1 to 7.9) are the suggested NLE team neuro-actionables based on the characteristics of each Enneagram dimension. Each dimension taps into the strengths or nuances of that Enneagram. This means if the team profile is strong in certain Enneagram focuses, likely the team will find it easier or more natural to do these neuro-actionables. If the team profile is weak in certain Enneagram focuses, the team may consider implementing some of the interventions in that dimension to balance or complement their tendencies, even if it feels less instinctive. For instance, a team profile of 1-5-3 that exhibits low affinity in Enneagram Four might need to intentionally incorporate creativity into their workflows. A practical approach for such a team could involve establishing a structured brainstorming process to actively encourage innovative thinking and emotional connection, rather than relying on spontaneous or organic methods.

Dimension	Team Neuro-Actionables
Mindset	• Emphasise vision, mission, core values, or higher objectives whenever possible (e.g. meetings, town hall, etc.) • Make key or tough decisions that are aligned with the higher purpose or core values
Dialogue	• Conduct Alignment Dialogue that bridges individual effort to the team purpose • Mediate conflicts, focusing on what is useful towards alignment to the higher purpose or main objectives
Actions	• Establish operating principles that guide team direction • Develop or co-create rules of engagement within the team and across teams to drive alignment

Table 7.1: Enneagram One Focus—Drive Team Alignment.

Dimension	Team Neuro-Actionables
Mindset	• Emphasise constructive conflicts and feedback, allowing differing perspectives and views to enrich discussions • Consult people who are impacted by the decisions in the decision-making process to elicit concerns and create early buy-in
Dialogue	• Conduct Empathic Dialogue that focuses on needs, understanding, and appreciation • Conduct regular one-to-one sessions to build trust and understanding at the personal level (not just at the professional level)
Actions	• Create platforms for the team to interact, reflect and understand • Provide constructive and direct feedback systems with support

Table 7.2: Enneagram Two Focus—Build Connections and Understanding.

Dimension	Team Neuro-Actionables
Mindset	• Emphasise creating a positive impact through a commitment to results • Focus on defining the rationale ("Why") and the desired outcomes and results ("What"), instead of telling people the steps and processes ("How")
Dialogue	• Conduct Accountability Dialogue that is respectful and supportive • When things do not go as planned, ask about the impact and implications, and discuss catchup plans
Actions	• Set effective goals or meaningful metrics with periodic follow-through • Establish a resource allocation framework to set aside proper resourcing

Table 7.3: Enneagram Three Focus—Drive Performance Excellence.

Dimension	Team Neuro-Actionables
Mindset	• Emphasise creating trust and enhancing the team culture • Identify "coachable moments" in team interactions to bring forth the importance of trust and culture
Dialogue	• Conduct Authentic Dialogue that allows individuals to express themselves and make personal connections to the team goals/vision • Create reflection opportunities for team members to go inward to take up self-responsibility that will drive trust with others and enhance team dynamics
Actions	• Create platforms for creative inputs or ideation; build on one another's ideas in meetings and discussions • Establish platforms for appreciation of both the team and individuals in a personal way

Table 7.4: Enneagram Four Focus—Build Trust and Culture.

Dimension	Team Neuro-Actionables
Mindset	• Emphasise driving in-depth mastery and holistic learning that contribute to the team's performance • Use data in decision-making to complement gut feel or experience
Dialogue	• Conduct Technical Dialogue that promotes deep learning and mentoring • Share and teach technical learning and insights in layman's terms to bridge understanding within the team
Actions	• Co-create creative solutions or deep problem-solving together • Develop data management systems to capture and share information more effectively

Table 7.5: Enneagram Five Focus—Develop Learning and Insights.

Dimension	Team Neuro-Actionables
Mindset	• Emphasise developing frameworks, systems, and processes that enable effective team dynamic • Focus on imparting intention, rationale, and thought processes instead of just listing the steps and to-dos for deeper understanding
Dialogue	• Conduct Stewardship Dialogue that encourages people to take the lead, build communities, and decentralise ownership • Challenge systems and processes and ask difficult questions to ensure the support systems continue to serve the objectives and vision
Actions	• Establish project management and planning methodologies for effective change management • Develop evaluation criteria, change indicators, transition, and risk mitigation plans for successful pivoting or planning

Table 7.6: Enneagram Six Focus—Drive Stewardship and Processes.

Dimension	Team Neuro-Actionables
Mindset	• Emphasise solutioning and creativity • Apply an Agile mindset and methodology to new or unfamiliar undertakings
Dialogue	• Conduct Exploratory Dialogue that encourages ideation, storytelling, and experimentation • Conduct AAR (Action-After-Review) or post-mortem to distil learning and insights into experimentation
Actions	• Create brainstorming, ideation, and idea curation processes and platforms • Train and develop team members on facilitation skills

Table 7.7: Enneagram Seven Focus—Unlock Potential and Possibilities.

Dimension	Team Neuro-Actionables
Mindset	• Emphasise personal growth and team development (growth mindset) • Focus on balancing stretching versus stabilising with individuals to develop them in a sustainable way (prevent burnout)
Dialogue	• Conduct Growth Dialogue that pushes the team from the comfort zone into the stretch zone • Conduct "difficult conversations" within the team to address the "elephant in the room"
Actions	• Create platforms for challenging ideas, assumptions, hypotheses, and thinking models • Develop talents in a structured manner through stretched assignments, mentoring, and coaching

Table 7.8: Enneagram Eight Focus—Drive Growth.

Dimension	Team Neuro-Actionables
Mindset	• Emphasise sustainability growth by building synergies through win-win collaboration • Identify touchpoints and opportunities to be inclusive and collaborative within and outside the team
Dialogue	• Conduct Partnership Dialogue that drives collaboration and synergy • Communicate in an inclusive manner and create a safe space for everyone to express and contribute to diversity
Actions	• Nurture collaborative initiatives for mid-term and long-term balance • Establish team rituals and routines to build pride and team identity

Table 7.9: Enneagram Nine Focus—Develop Synergies.

The integration of team neuro-actionables offers a promising avenue for organisations to foster a healthy team dynamic that supports a high-performing team culture. Applying them to team management together with leadership development and organisational interventions, organisations can create a conducive environment that supports the holistic development and well-being of teams while driving business success. With a thoughtful and strategic approach to implementing team neuro-actionables, organisations can unlock the full potential of their teams and achieve sustainable growth and competitiveness in the ever-evolving business landscape.

In the subsequent chapters, we shall see how team profiles can be used together with team neuro-actionables in each context.

Chapter 8

CASE STUDY: LEADERSHIP ONBOARDING

BACKGROUND

Gwen managed a small-medium-sized e-commerce enterprise with approximately 120 employees. Recently, she recruited a Chief Operating Officer (COO) to assist in the company's expansion and process enhancement. This case study delves into how an HR consultant, utilising the NLE Team Profile, aided Gwen in devising a customised onboarding strategy for Brian, the new COO, based on his specific profile, to ensure his successful integration.

Brian's profile was 3-8-5 (see figure 8.1), characterised by a self-motivated, self-assured individual with a keen emphasis on achieving tangible outcomes. Gwen was convinced of this initial impression during her interview with Brian, and his directness and results-oriented approach were key factors in his hiring. She sought someone of his calibre to drive operational efficiency and streamline internal processes. In essence, she needed a strong problem-solver.

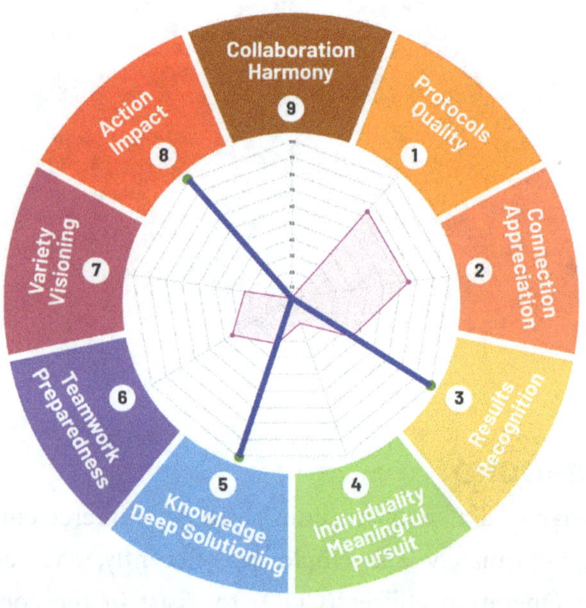

Figure 8.1: Team Map—Brian: 3-8-5 / Team: 1-2-6.

Brian brought with him eight years of pertinent industry experience, including five years of people management expertise. His rapid career progression was attributed to his drive and ability to deliver tangible results. Opting to join Gwen's SME, he aimed to gain greater exposure to business and strategic endeavours. At 32 years old, Brian harboured ambitions of contributing to the growth of a company and advancing into senior leadership roles. Concurrently, he pursued an MBA to further augment his skill set.

Jen, the HR consultant, learnt of Brian's recruitment when Gwen informed her about the impending organisational restructuring and alterations to reporting lines. Upon realising the significance of Brian's role, which would encompass overseeing all operations and procurement upon his arrival, Jen decided to conduct a comprehensive profile assessment. The purpose was to develop a tailored onboarding plan that would facilitate Brian's seamless integration and success from the outset, a suggestion that Gwen welcomed wholeheartedly.

ANALYSIS AND INSIGHTS

Jen possessed not only Brian's profile but also the profiles of the operations and procurement teams. The consolidated team profile showed a 1-2-6 configuration (figure 8.1). Based on this, she provided the following advice and analysis to Gwen using both Team Maps and 4PP Spectrums (see figure 8.2, overleaf).

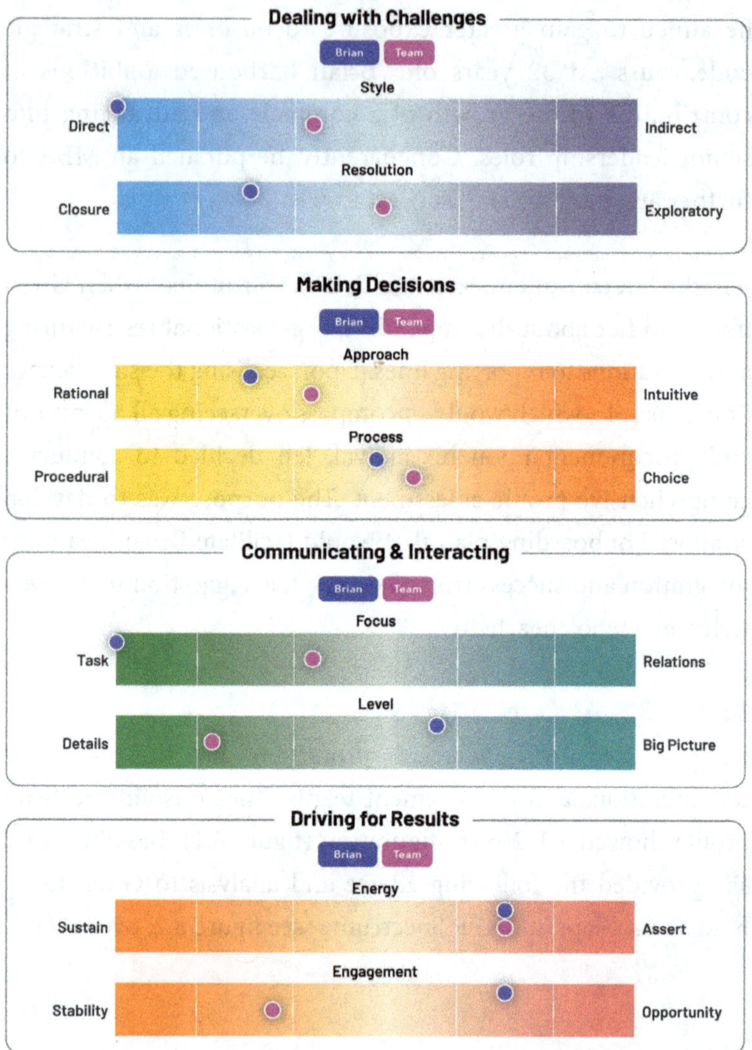

Figure 8.2: 4PP Spectrum: Brian: 3-8-5 / Team: 1-2-6.

Ways in which Brian would contribute to the team:

- Brian's directness and urgency aligned with the team's decision-making style and objectives for change.
- His ability to balance the big picture and details would guide the team toward a strategic focus.
- Brian's knack for spotting opportunities would inspire the team to achieve change outcomes effectively.

Ways in which Brian might encounter tensions with the team:

- Brian's strong desire to prove his competence might lead to overlooking relationship-building with key stakeholders.
- His directness in addressing inefficiencies could negatively impact team morale and relationships.
- Brian's focus on results might clash with the team's problem-focused approach, appearing confrontational.

ACTIONS AND RESULTS

Understanding the potential challenges and benefits of Brian's profile, Gwen collaborated with Jen to design a comprehensive onboarding plan. In addition to the standard orientation programme, they implemented the following:

First thirty days:

- Established benchmarks for Growth Conversations and communicated the success metrics for the COO role, so that Brian has clarity on how his success would be measured.
- Introduced Brian to key stakeholders with a focus on building effective relationships as part of his KPIs, so that Brian will focus on people and relationships.

- Communicated to Brian that his confirmation would depend on feedback from key stakeholders to support the above KPI.
- Guided Brian on seeking Gwen's involvement to ensure a successful start, so that Brian knows when to ask for support, and not perceive seeking help as failure.

To prepare the team for Brian's arrival, Gwen began communicating the change vision and objectives, ensuring they understood that the change was an organisational decision. Gwen also solicited support from senior team members to facilitate Brian's onboarding.

Instead of assigning the standard "two-week buddy" from the team, Gwen ensured that Brian had a mentor (the CFO) at the peer level for three months. This approach helped Brian establish peer relationships, recognise the CFO's seniority and partnership, and gain insights into the business's commercial aspects.

Gwen engaged with Brian weekly to provide guidance and support for the first 30 days and subsequently, fortnightly for the remaining period.

In the following months:

- Gwen reviewed Brian's progress based on the success criteria.
- She provided direct and respectful feedback to help him enhance his performance.
- Brian was encouraged to communicate "bad news" as well as "good news" to facilitate proactive planning.
- Gwen sought Brian's observations and integrated his opinions into the change plan.

- Jen facilitated team bonding events and an alignment workshop with a focus on Change as the theme.

After three months, Brian seamlessly integrated with the team, showcasing a higher level of maturity and stability than initially anticipated. He later shared that the explicit guidance from various stakeholders had greatly aided his orientation and facilitated his assimilation into the organisational culture. Interestingly, he noted that it was the first time in his career that he had been explicitly advised not to rush into making immediate changes. Surprisingly, this directive granted him the opportunity and the mind space to observe and learn at an accelerated pace.

Gwen's preparatory efforts were instrumental in setting the stage for these changes. Consequently, the team did not perceive Brian as the catalyst for disruptive changes, and Brian felt that the shared context of change became a collective goal to strive for, fostering a unified team spirit. Leveraging his comprehensive perspective, Brian adeptly communicated the underlying purpose of the changes, highlighting the team's direct contributions to the overall change objectives.

With Brian's eye for results and enthusiasm, he celebrated quick wins within the team, fostering camaraderie and making the change journey enjoyable. Gwen was delighted as she could delegate operational tasks to Brian, enabling her to focus on expanding the business.

The case study highlights the importance of a tailored onboarding plan that leverages the leader's profile and promotes a smooth transition while ensuring successful integration and effective team dynamics.

Chapter 9

CASE STUDY: UNLOCKING TEAM CONVERSATIONS

BACKGROUND

Dan, the founder of this fintech start-up, initiated the venture three years ago, and the company has experienced steady growth since its inception. Bolstered by a recent Series A funding round, Dan now envisions expanding the company's presence across more cities in Southeast Asia, necessitating the scaling of his leadership team.

Despite having successfully assembled a competent team that collaborates effectively, Dan anticipates that the impending scale-up will subject the team's operations to significant stress and challenges. While he senses that there are recurring operational issues persisting within the various divisions, their exact nature and location elude precise identification.

As the year drew to a close, Dan seized the opportunity to celebrate by taking a proactive step. Recognising the need for a deeper understanding of his team's dynamics, he engaged an external facilitator to conduct a team profile. Through this facilitated team conversation, Dan aimed to unearth valuable insights that could illuminate the path toward resolving operational challenges and fortifying the team for the upcoming expansion.

ANALYSIS AND INSIGHTS

Upon grasping the provided context, facilitator Sarah opted to leverage the NLE Team Profile as a tool to guide the team conversation.

Upon generating the NLE Team Profile, the resulting configuration was 2-5-3 (as depicted in figure 9.1).

Figure 9.1: Team Profile 2-5-3.

This profile revealed a spectrum of characteristics:

- Type Two dimension emphasised relationships, care, connection, and empathy. Under stress, the team might form cliques, become overly subjective, and prioritise relationships over results.
- Type Five dimension focused on learning, in-depth problem-solving, technicality, and objectivity. Stress might lead the team to become excessively task-oriented, potentially contradicting the Type Two dimension. They could also become cynical and withdraw support and participation.
- Type Three dimension prioritised results, efficiency, success, and tasks. Under stress, the team might avoid failure, engage

in excessive internal competition, and undermine each other's contributions and achievements.

Identifying numerous potential tension points within the team, Sarah recognised that their primary challenge might centre around conflict resolution and effective accountability. However, Dan's description suggested that, despite these potential issues, the team functioned well together. This indicated a foundation of trust and established relations over time.

Approaching the situation with her characteristic blend of scepticism and extensive experience as a consultant and facilitator, Sarah began to discern why the team's productivity might be falling short with recurring challenges.

ACTIONS AND RESULTS

On the actual day of the workshop, Sarah arrived early at the training room to observe the team right from the beginning. As team members streamed in, she noticed their strong personal connections, with everyone acknowledging each other warmly. The room quickly filled with enthusiasm and friendliness, setting a positive tone for the day. While this was a promising start, Sarah quietly pondered the value she could add to the team that, on the surface, appeared perfect.

The Team Profile discussion, however, proved illuminating. Sarah observed that the team's conversations tended to stay on the surface, reflecting good intentions to be considerate and mindful of others' feelings. This likely mirrored their daily interactions, where issues were gently raised, and if unresolved, swept under the bridge. Sarah raised her observations and skilfully prompted the team to unveil key challenges:

- The team appreciated Dan's efforts in shielding them from the board and securing funding. However, they tended to handle issues at their level, even when involving Dan might be more effective.
- Concerned about Dan's well-being, the team hesitated to hold him accountable when he fell short on promises, opting to explore alternative solutions silently.
- Dan, acknowledging the team's hard work, was reluctant to fully delegate, inadvertently becoming the bottleneck in decision-making and causing inefficiencies.
- Dan's reluctance to hold the team accountable at times had further implications.

In essence, the team prioritised preserving relations at the expense of performance, solving broken promises individually rather than through dialogue, leading to missed synergies and suboptimal productivity. The team realised that while managing the current stress level, they were depleting the trust bank account. With impending hires and increased pressure, the account was at risk of bankruptcy once the business scaled up. The team grappled with visualising how to balance both performance and relationships.

Sarah delved into the 4PP Spectrums (see figure 9.2, overleaf) and offered actionable tips:

- Monthly regrouping to reprioritise strategic objectives and hold each other accountable for the greater good.
- Communicating decision-making criteria to avoid surprises and improve understanding.

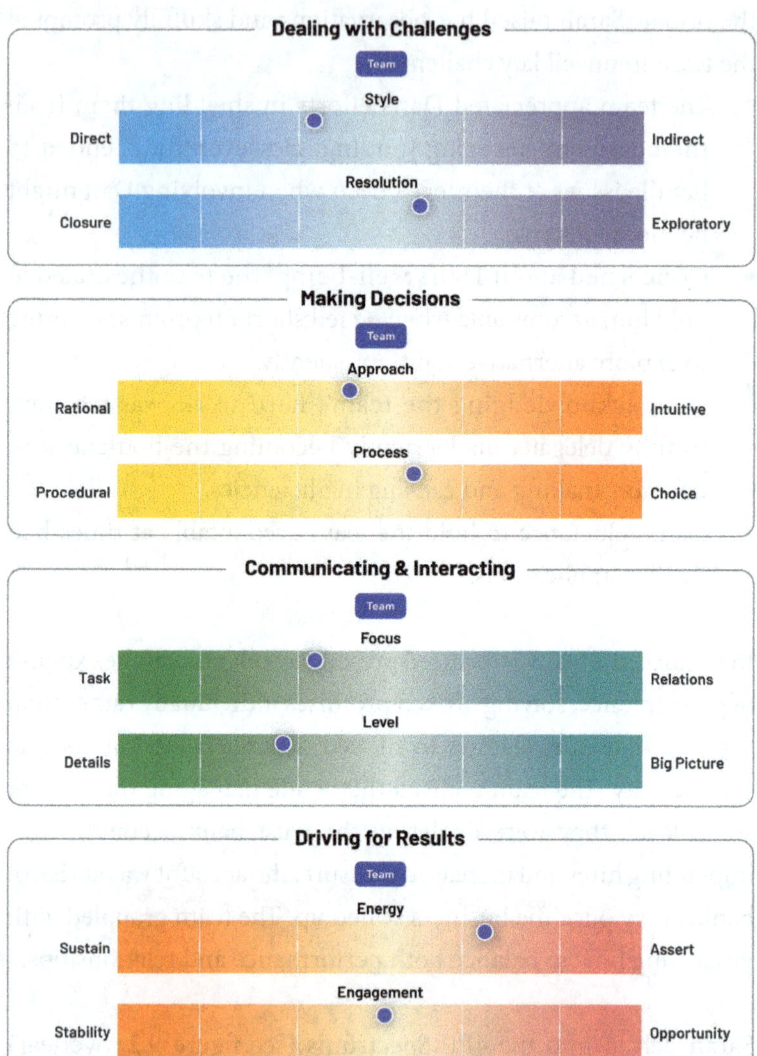

Figure 9.2: 4PP Spectrums—Team Profile 2-5-3.

- Recognising accountability as a means to foster trust, understanding, and camaraderie.
- Focusing on discussing impact and implications tied to strategic objectives.

The team initially viewed accountability negatively, akin to penalisation. Sarah clarified that accountability conversations were essential for leadership, directly impacting performance and building trust and commitment. Excited to apply their new-found insights, the team promptly booked Sarah for the next workshop on the Effective Accountability programme.

This case study highlighted how a Team Profile facilitated discussions about the "invisible" dynamic, bridging understanding and fostering solutions and alignment. It showcased the courage of a performing team to introspect and improve, recognising that even success required continuous thoughtful management to avoid setbacks.

Chapter 10

CASE STUDY: RESTRUCTURING

BACKGROUND

A few months after the merger and acquisition, ripple effects permeated the organisation's back-end operations. While the front-end product lines and branding remained unchanged due to complexity and market sentiments, a restructuring of back-end units, from procurement to corporate services, was underway. Mabel, the CFO of the parent company (acquirer), assumed the leadership of the upcoming streamlining project, tasked with merging the two finance teams and integrating the subsidiary finance team into the Group Finance consisting of 32 people.

The challenge lay in integrating eight people from the acquired finance team, whose structure, systems, and processes significantly differed from those of the Group, a listed company. Retaining the expertise and personnel of this team was paramount, given their manual processes, technical product lines, and the critical knowledge residing within the team. Moreover, integration would introduce additional financial reporting and complexity.

The acquired team, tightly knit under the leadership of Senior Finance Manager Chris, faced a significant shift. Each team member had been with Chris for more than three years, and their response to the change would be influenced by her cues. Mabel, cautious about approaching Chris, was uncertain about how best to navigate this situation.

Seeking guidance, Mabel consulted her HR business partner, Lee, a certified practitioner in the NLE Team profiling tool. Lee suggested using the NLE Team Profile to gain insights into the best approach for the integration. Mabel discussed her intentions with Chris, who agreed to proceed with the plan.

ANALYSIS AND INSIGHTS

Lee conducted individual profiling for both the Group Finance team and the eight members of the acquired finance team, resulting in Team Profiles (figure 10.1): Group Finance with a profile of 1-3-6 and the acquired finance team with a profile of 5-4-6.

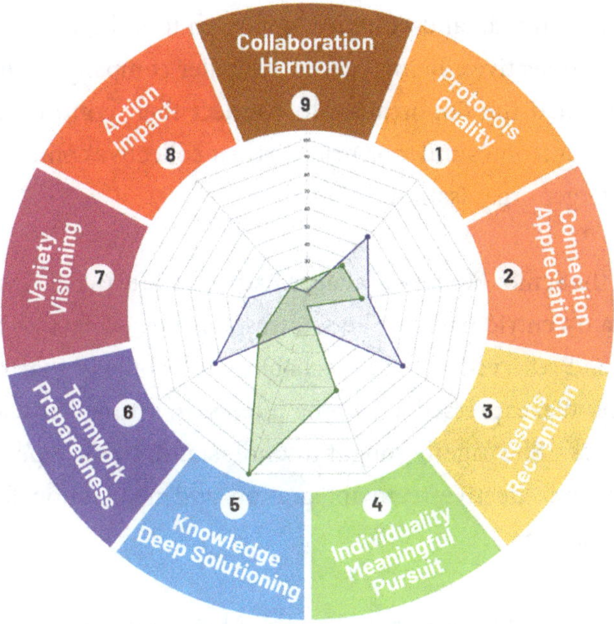

Figure 10.1: Team Profile—Group 1-3-6 / 8-Pax 5-4-6.

The Group Finance profile of 1-3-6 suggested a more structured, procedural, process-oriented, and competency-driven team. Their operations were well-documented, transacted, and systemised, adhering to the necessary level of governance and reporting, complemented by the Shared Services operations structure. Additionally, the Group Finance team boasted a robust ERP (Enterprise Resource Planning) system, ensuring efficient automation.

In contrast, the acquired finance team profile of 5-4-6, coupled with more manual operations, signalled that problem-solving could be more individual-led than systemised. The team tended to adopt a "divide-and-conquer" approach to tasks, aligned with strategic objectives. Being part of a smaller company, each team member had the opportunity to connect their contribution to business outcomes and took pride in their collective contributions to the larger organisation.

Chris, the Senior Finance Manager, had a profile of 6-1-5, revealing her team-centric nature. She was responsible, protective of her team, and reserved but approachable. Chris, openly sharing her team profile, expressed a genuine interest in setting her team up for success. She eagerly sought to understand the Group's profile to facilitate effective team integration and negotiation for her team members.

Upon reviewing both team profiles, Mabel and Chris shared a common concern about the integration process. The acquired finance team would likely need to be divided into specialised functions, reporting to different subunit managers. This restructuring would disrupt their strong sense of belonging to the current team. Chris recognised the need to communicate with each team member individually, helping them make decisions aligned with their best career interests.

Lee, having some reservations about Chris' profile, shared her concerns during her profile debriefing with Mabel. Leaders with a Type 6 profile could sometimes be overly protective of their teams, potentially at the expense of the larger organisation. With this in mind, Mabel discussed with Chris the importance of convincing the team to stay for at least a year post-integration for a win-win outcome. This approach allowed the team to experience their new roles before deciding on long-term career choices, either within or outside the Group, ensuring the stability of the integration. Chris agreed to this approach, emphasising that the ultimate decision would rest with the individual team members, but she would try her best to retain them.

ACTIONS AND RESULTS

Informed by the insights from the team and individual profile, Mabel made the strategic decision to have Chris co-lead the integration alongside her, providing a reassurance presence for the acquired team. Chris, displaying a deep commitment to her team, assumed the responsibility of ensuring their smooth transition into the new structure and expanded roles. She pledged to continue coaching and mentoring the team for a year, even as they transitioned out of her direct reporting line. The team, valuing Chris' leadership, openly shared their concerns with her, facilitating effective collaboration between Mabel and Chris to address these issues.

Capitalising on this opportunity, Mabel undertook a process optimisation initiative within the Group, enhancing clarity and purposefulness. This involved consolidating reporting formats, incorporating more strategic metrics, and refining operational meeting agendas to include pertinent business updates. These improvements allowed Group Finance to better understand their contributions to financial and commercial management and reporting. Although Chris initially faced challenges adjusting to the corporate environment and managing diverse stakeholder requests, with Mabel's guidance and support, she quickly earned respect from stakeholders within the Group.

The integration proved to be a success, with seven team members choosing to stay, and only one person opting to pursue further studies a year post-integration. Recognising Chris's exceptional leadership, she was promoted to Finance Director 15 months later, taking on responsibilities in management reporting and leading the Shared Services operations under Mabel's guidance.

This case exemplifies how team profiles can be instrumental in post-merger and acquisition scenarios or any restructuring involving the combination of teams. The insights derived from the profiles not only guided leaders in their approach to the integration but also fostered mutual appreciation between the teams, reframing perceived differences as valuable distinctions rather than obstacles.

Chapter 11

CASE STUDY: CHANGE MANAGEMENT

BACKGROUND

Matt, serving as the Chief Human Resources Officer (CHRO) in an engineering and construction company, played a pivotal role in the steering committee overseeing a multimillion-dollar digital transformation project. Within this initiative, Matt identified three crucial divisions that demanded his focused attention due to their political dynamics and strategic implications: the Subcontractors (Subcon) division, the Sales division, and the Contracts division.

Heading the Subcon division was Shawn, the Executive Director, who proved to be the most hesitant sponsor of the project. Expressing scepticism, Shawn believed that the existing processes were effective and doubted the promised return on investment (ROI), anticipating additional workload and staffing requirements for his already lean team. While he outwardly cooperated in steering committee meetings, he engaged in numerous side conversations expressing his reservations and frustrations. Matt faced challenges influencing Shawn due to their past strained relationship.

Jeremy, the Sales Director, led the Sales division, struggling with adherence to internal deadlines, processes, and company rules. His priorities leaned heavily towards customer-centric tasks, potentially causing delays in handling system-related aspects crucial for both presales and post-sales activities. The impact of Jeremy's cooperation was substantial, influencing the subsequent processing of construction projects and affecting the entire company.

In charge of the Contracts division was Kyle, an experienced Contracts Director overseeing procurement and shipment processes. Managing contractual terms, bill-of-materials quantity calculations, and inventory management, Kyle led a sizeable team of 18 people because of their reliance on Excel spreadsheets. The digital transformation project posed a significant challenge for her, as its implementation would drastically reduce her team's size. Emotionally attached to her team, which she had nurtured from scratch, Kyle found it difficult to accept the impending changes. Despite understanding the project's benefits, she struggled with the emotional impact on her loyal, yet potentially unadaptable, team members, making their redeployment post-implementation a challenging prospect for Matt.

ANALYSIS AND INSIGHTS

Recognising the importance of effectively managing resistance in the ongoing digital transformation project, Matt, an experienced change agent, enlisted an experienced facilitator, Karen, particularly her expertise to conduct team profiles for the three divisions. The aim was to identify team tendencies and formulate a change strategy that aligns with each team's characteristics.

Subcon Profile: 1-7-6

The team profile of 1-7-6 for the Subcon team (figure 11.1, overleaf) indicates a preference for detail-oriented and procedural approaches, showcasing a desire for control and methodical planning and execution. Operating within the fragmented and relational Subcon industry, the team's resourcefulness is crucial as they tap into their network to find alternatives and diverse sources of materials and negotiate effectively with the Main Contractor (Maincon) customers.

Figure 11.1: Subcon Team Profile 1-7-6.

In response to change, their 4PP Spectrums profile (see figure 11.2) highlights these characteristics:

- This team tends to be direct in calling out issues (although it might be in a sceptical or complaining way);
- A need to understand how the change will enhance their job performance;
- A desire to be consulted and have a say in the change plan or its execution;
- A focus on improvement, aiming to "do better" in their current responsibilities with ample support;
- A preference for being informed, seeking certainty, and valuing consistency; thus, providing a heads-up is crucial.

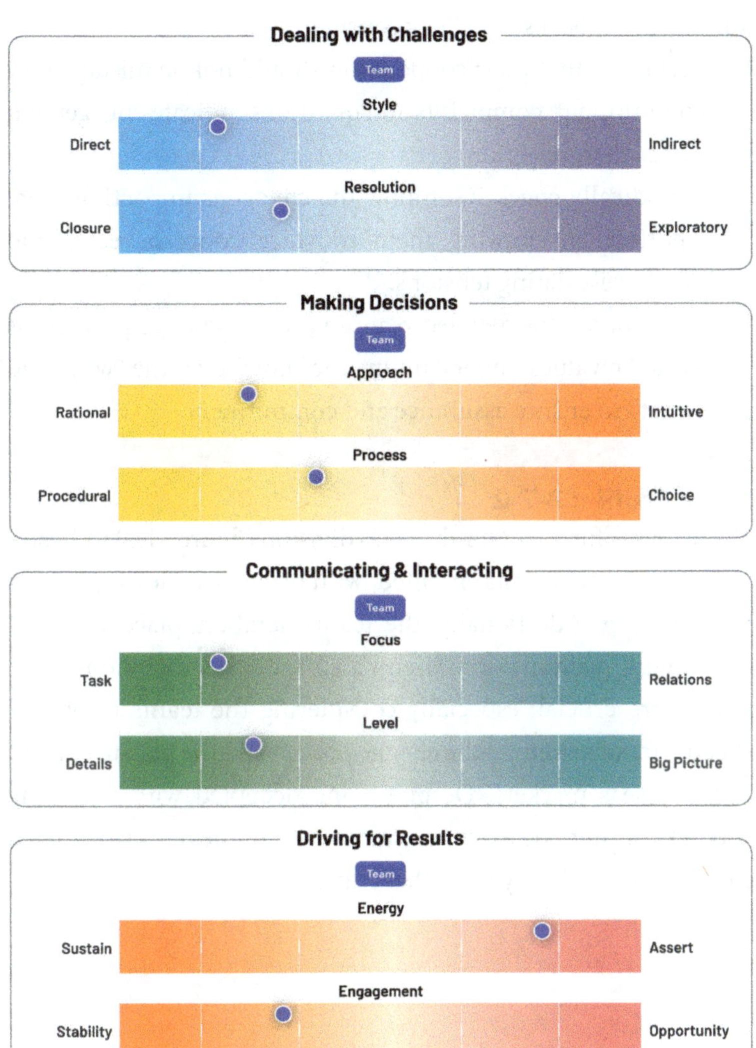

Figure 11.2: 4PP Spectrums—Subcon Team Profile 1-7-6.

Karen emphasised several key considerations:

- Recognise that their cooperation should not be mistaken for commitment; complaints and questions indicate engagement rather than rejection.
- Periodically check in on how the change is impacting them emotionally, allowing them to voice concerns early and prevent escalating tensions.
- Be prepared for detailed planning in the change process, as the team values understanding the "how" over the "why" and "what" to ensure assurance and commitment.

Sales Profile: 3-7-2

The team profile 3-7-2 for the Sales division (figure 11.3) indicates a focus on being results-oriented, with pride in achieving success and winning. Additionally, the team members place value on meaningful relationships. Jeremy's attitude and direction of the project are crucial, especially considering the team's busy year ahead—involvement in the change project and the plan to expand into overseas markets. Despite being occupied with tendering and networking, the extended sales cycles in the highly regulated construction industry pose challenges.

Figure 11.3: Sales Team Profile 3-7-2.

In response to change, the Sales team exhibits the following characteristics from the 4PP Spectrums (figure 11.4, overleaf):

- Flexibility and adaptability to changes;
- Quick decision-making, subject to spontaneous adjustment if priorities are not committed;
- High energy and openness to changes, particularly if they bring better rewards and recognition;
- Proactiveness in making things happen, coupled with eagerness to explore new opportunities.

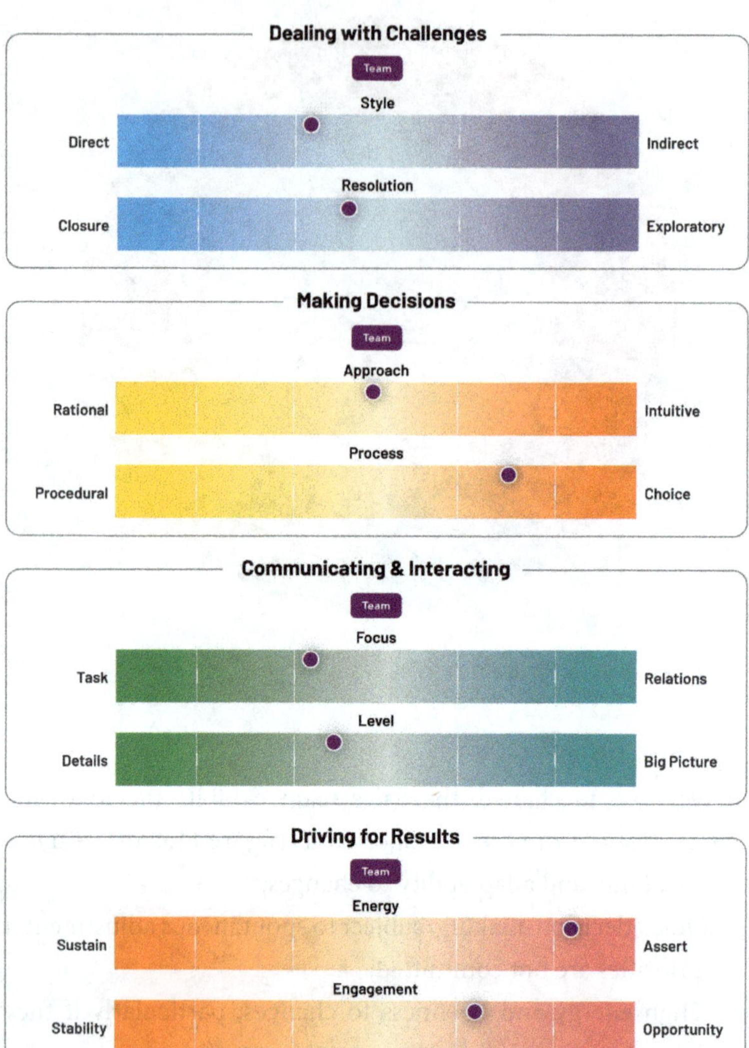

Figure 11.4: 4PP Spectrums— Sales Team Profile 3-7-2.

Karen emphasised several key considerations:

- Inspire the team with a compelling vision and clear change outcomes tied to the reward structure to motivate them effectively.
- Integrate clear success and progress metrics into their year-end KPIs to instil a sense of urgency and importance.
- Provide support in handling administrative and process details to ensure the project timeline is met.
- Show appreciation and recognition for the team's progress, as this is vital to Jeremy and the entire team.

Contracts Profile: 9-1-5

This profile 9-1-5 for the Contracts division (figure 11.5, overleaf) indicates a focus on compliance, methodical approaches, and attention to detail. Given the administrative nature of the division, the team excels in strong follow-through, patience, conscientiousness, and providing excellent support to the Maincon, Subcon, and Finance divisions in all projects.

Figure 11.5: Contracts Team Profile 9-1-5.

However, the introduction of the digital transformation project has induced stress within the team as numerous processes need to be changed and streamlined. The team's profile also suggests potential challenges in adaptability to changes and planning.

In response to change, the Contracts team exhibits the following characteristics based on the 4PP Spectrums (figure 11.6):

- Difficulty prioritising key objectives from various stakeholders without clear or aligned strategic intent;
- Need for a clear action plan with detailed execution guidelines;
- Value placed on working harmony, indicating that a structured conflict resolution platform or anonymous feedback may be crucial to address tensions and disagreements;
- Strong emphasis on doing things well and valuing competency.

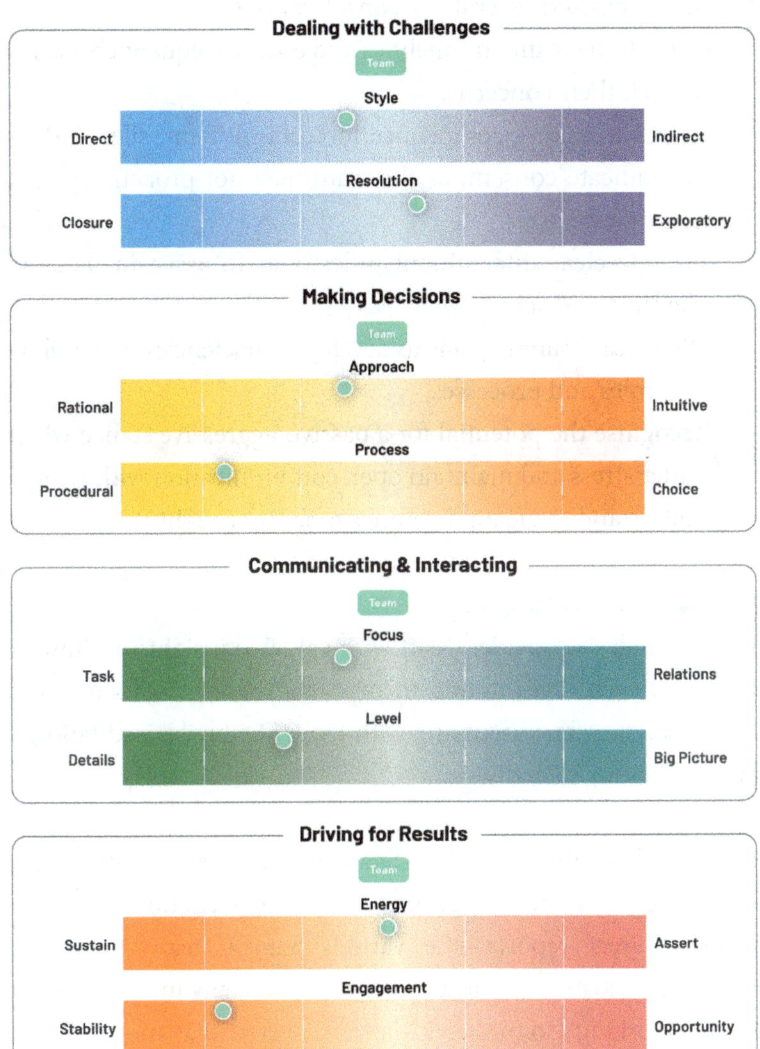

Figure 11.6: 4PP Spectrums—Contracts Team Profile 9-1-5.

Karen emphasised several key considerations:

- Consult the team on timelines and ensure frequent check-ins to elicit their concerns;
- Avoid mistaking compliance for commitment; silence does not indicate consent, as the team may not proactively seek help or support;
- Provide clear intermittent milestones to assist in detailed planning and scheduling;
- Offer clear training plans to develop competencies in handling new roles and processes;
- Recognise the potential for a passive-aggressive stance when under stress and maintain open communication with Kyle to understand the team dynamics more thoroughly.

ACTIONS AND RESULTS

Karen's analysis provided Matt with valuable insights on how to approach each division and incorporate these insights into the change plan. After discussing with the CEO, he devised tailored approaches for each division.

For the Subcon division, where Shawn's resistance was anticipated, Matt recognised the importance of building relationships with Shawn's direct reports—the various Subcon team managers. Leveraging existing connections and intentionally involving them in the Working Committee, Matt discovered that most Subcon team managers welcomed the change. They saw the potential for improved industry competitiveness, better planning, and enhanced accuracy in labour and equipment scheduling—all could result in better profit margins. This commercial angle provided Matt with valuable insights to position the change effectively.

In the Sales division, recent losses had impacted morale—they had lost three pitches consecutively in the last five months. Matt had a personal conversation with Jeremy, emphasising that excelling in the digital transformation project could be a quick win for the team, especially in light of the challenges of winning external deals. Jeremy acknowledged the significance of internal project success for the team's morale and saw it as an opportunity to score points for his year-end evaluation.

For the Contracts division, workload, adaptability, and competency were primary concerns. Recognising the significant impact of the transformation project on this division, Matt decided to bring in a Six-Sigma Lean Consultant to work with Kyle on process improvement. This external expertise was crucial in mitigating the workload—alleviating the team's pressure to think beyond their current processes, and a detailed skills mapping exercise helped develop a customised training plan for the team.

The digital transformation project concluded successfully, despite some delays. The Subcon division experienced notable improvements in costing and scheduling, leading to a steady increase in profit margins in the next 18 months and increased competitiveness in the industry due to better planning. The Sales division completed its project ahead of schedule, but enforcement of timely input of data into the system remained a challenge for the first nine months after the project ended and when sales picked up. The Contracts division benefited from external expertise, had reduced stress and confusion. The project resulted in a reduction of five headcounts, with three team members transitioning well into new processes and roles and the loss of two team members joining smaller competitors.

This case underscores how understanding team dynamics and utilising team profiles strategically can mitigate resistance to change, complementing and contributing to the overarching change management process.

Chapter 12

CASE STUDY: TEAM COACHING

BACKGROUND

Wilson eagerly anticipated the upcoming year as he concluded the funding round with a new injection of US$2.5 million. This financial boost allowed him to expedite business scaling and double the headcount within the next 12 months. Recognising the critical role of an optimised leadership team dynamic in achieving this ambitious goal, Wilson sought the expertise of a team coach.

A year ago, Wilson's 12-member leadership team engaged Therese, a leadership coach and trainer, for a comprehensive Leadership

Programme consisting of 10 modules. The programme equipped the team with essential leadership skills, including effective feedback, delegation, and accountability, and a session to draw the team charter. These acquired skills and mindsets fostered greater cohesion, deepened understanding, and built stronger trust within the leadership team.

With the introduction of stretch goals, a new strategy, and larger teams to lead in the next 12 months, the leadership team recognised the need for additional support. They aimed to ensure that key priorities were consistently pursued, important decisions were made with efficacy, and the team's unit remained intact. Acknowledging the significant impact of senior leadership on organisational culture, Therese was enlisted to coach the team during their monthly management meetings.

Drawing on the foundation laid during the Leadership Programme, Therese instilled key leadership principles and mindsets while developing simple frameworks for effective communication within the team. After observing one of their meetings, Therese identified suboptimal team dynamics and numerous missed opportunities for more effective collaboration, such as soliciting everyone's input, responding constructively to ideas, and asking insightful questions. Recognising these coachable moments, she proposed the concept of ongoing team coaching to Wilson, who agreed that it was a timely intervention.

ANALYSIS AND INSIGHTS

Therese conducted a profiling of the leadership team during the program (see figure 12.1), revealing a 6-7-2 profile.

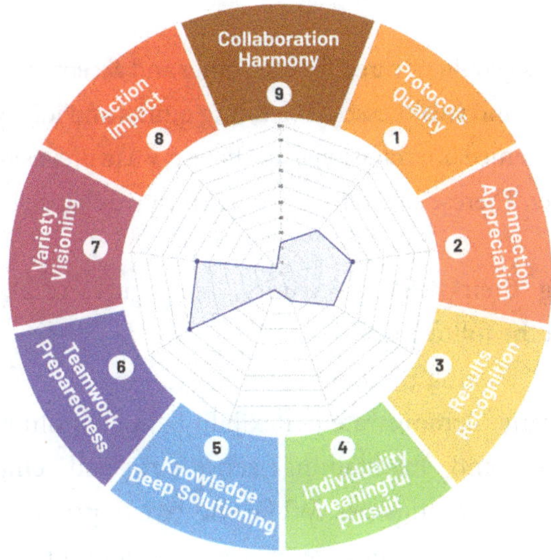

Figure 12.1: Team Profile 6-7-2.

Drawing on her working experience with the team, she identified a Responsive Dynamic (team health) characterised by several key traits:

- Strong Sense of Belonging
  The team exhibited a robust commitment to their mission to each other. They readily offered help to colleagues, engaged in collaborative problem-solving, and even advocated for team members who occasionally failed to deliver.
- Bonding Beyond Work
  Outside of official responsibilities, the team invested considerable time in bonding activities. Whether over drinks, meals, weekend sports, or personal events like housewarming and weddings, they fostered a positive and enjoyable atmosphere. Meetings were infused with banter and witty exchanges, alleviating the pressures of daily work.

- Genuine Care

  Members genuinely cared for each other and accepted each other's strengths and weaknesses. Tolerating quirks and idiosyncrasies, even if deemed unprofessional by Therese, was a prevalent practice. However, Therese aimed to encourage positive change in this area.

Examining their 4PP Spectrums (see figure 12.2), Therese confirmed the following:

- Problem-Solving Flexibility

  The team demonstrated flexibility in handling diverse problems and maintaining sensitivity and empathy in addressing certain issues. While effective in problem-solving, the team might not engage in deep, meaningful discussions. Problem-solving was often mistaken for learning.
- Decision-Making Agility

  Although capable of making various types of decisions, the team struggled with unclear decision ownership. Group consensus often took precedence, leading to safe decisions rather than optimal ones.
- Detail Orientation

  The team exhibited a detailed approach, sometimes structured and sometimes not. The penchant for detail occasionally resulted in lengthy, unfocused conversations, with meetings veering off-topic and extending beyond the allocated time.
- Accountability Challenges

  Proximity in relationships posed challenges in holding each other accountable. The team hesitated to challenge ideas, assumptions, or thought processes, preferring agreement over constructive critique. Issues perceived as "different" or "unique" were deferred, raising concerns about follow-through.

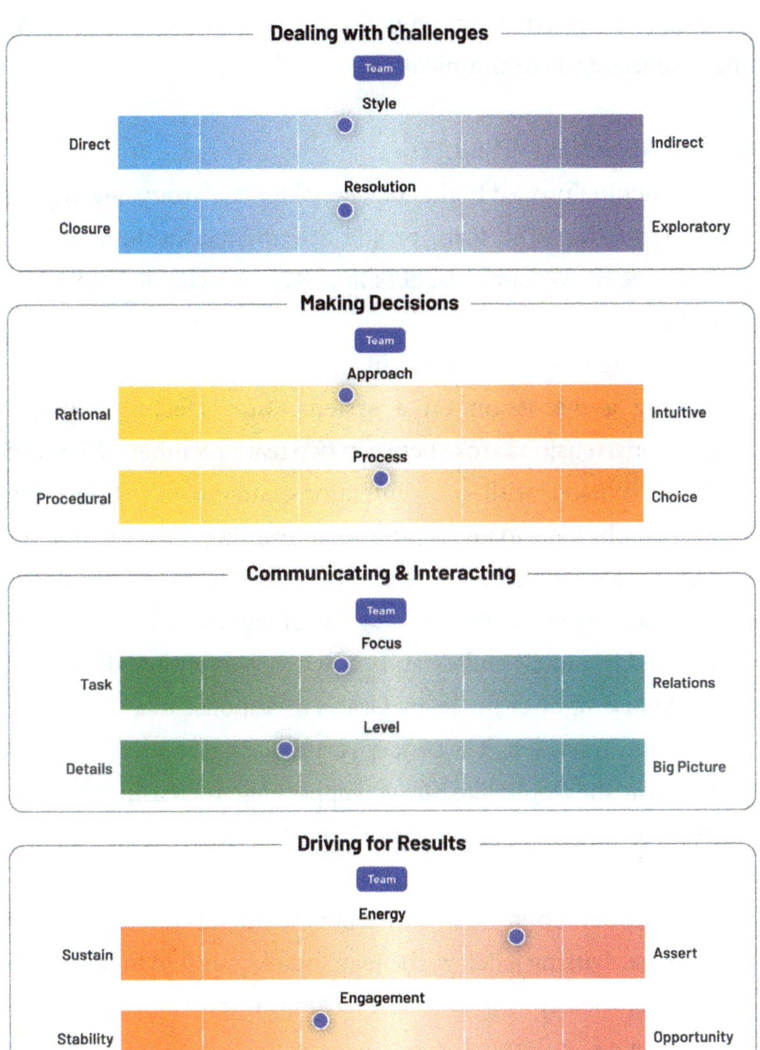

Figure 12.2: 4PP Spectrum—Team Profile 6-7-2.

Therese addressed these dynamics to enhance the team's effectiveness and communication.

ACTIONS AND RESULTS

Team coaching proved highly beneficial for the group, leveraging the insights from the team profile to enhance the four pivotal points under Wilson's leadership. Key coachable moments included:

- Clarifying Decision Ownership

  During a discussion on a system issue affecting multiple divisions, tensions arose between two team members, Max and Grace. Wilson, with good intentions, intervened by deciding on a solution, inadvertently undermining Grace's role as the decision owner. Therese's coaching questions prompted the team to objectively review the situation, clarify decision ownership, and understand how well-intentioned actions could disempower the team. Grace, in response to a thoughtful question, revealed her concerns, providing valuable insights and how she would like Max to support her, increasing the level of understanding regarding the issue on hand.
- Learning from Accountability

  In an accountability session, a team member, Dave, overlooked an issue, causing a delay. The team quickly shifted to problem-solving, nearly missing a learning opportunity. Therese intervened, guiding the team to explore the root cause. It emerged that a subordinate made a unilateral decision without informing Dave, highlighting a deeper leadership issue. The discussion delved into leadership principles and options for addressing the underlying problem before resolving the task delay, hence clearly segregating resolution from learning.

With team coaching, the leadership team engaged in profound conversations that strengthened trust and partnership while aligning with strategic objectives. They became more comfortable holding each other accountable, fostering a sense of mutual support and appreciation. This resulted in more effective decision-making and problem-solving.

The team members, through the team coaching process, gained valuable self-awareness, identifying obstacles, fears, potential leadership derailers, strengths, and synergies. They explored the transformative possibilities when stepping outside their comfort zones and engaging in deep conversations. They also learnt that leadership is a collective effort and does not lie with just the leader of the team.

Crucially, team coaching, coupled with the NLE Team Profile, made team dynamics visible and provided a shared reference point for everyone. Whatever behaviours exist in the team are endorsed (be it consciously or unconsciously) by everyone in the team. This empowered any team member to contribute to uplifting the dynamic, transforming leadership into a collective responsibility rather than solely relying on Wilson. The NLE Team Profile emerged as a powerful tool, demonstrating how understanding the team profile could enhance the effectiveness and direction of team coaching by establishing a shared language within the team.

AFTERWORD

After navigating the intricacies of team dynamics through the lens of the NLE Team Profile, we find ourselves at the culmination of a transformative journey. The stories shared within these pages unravel the profound impact that understanding team profiles can have on steering through the complexities of modern business landscapes.

As we bid farewell to the characters who graced these narratives—from Mabel orchestrating a financial integration to Matt navigating digital transformations, and Wilson propelling his vision forward—a collective wisdom emerges. The NLE Team Profile isn't merely a diagnostic tool; it becomes a compass, guiding leaders through unchartered territories.

In closing, it's imperative to recognise that the journey doesn't end here. The NLE Team Profile is a living, breathing entity within the fabric of organisations, continuously evolving as teams adapt, grow, and face new challenges. As leaders, the responsibility now lies in leveraging this new-found knowledge. It's an invitation to foster a culture of understanding, to bridge the gap between diverse team tendencies, and to embark on a journey of continuous improvement.

The stories shared are not just narratives; they are blueprints for leadership in a world where adaptability and cohesion are the cornerstones of success. As we turn the final page, let us carry forward the lessons learnt, armed with the realisation that the NLE Team Profile isn't just a tool—**it's a catalyst for transformative leadership and it is about installing leadership into teams**. The journey continues, and I hope to discover more success stories, contributions, and team-related work about Enneagram.

MIND TRANSFORMATIONS PTE LTD

Mind Transformations

We leverage research to empower the breakthrough and transformation you seek.

Mind Transformations Pte Ltd was established in 1997 by Dr Barney Wee and specialised in Neuro-linguistic Programming (NLP) programmes. Since then, we have expanded our range of programmes to Neuro-linguistic Enneagram (NLE) and Coaching, and have been conducting certification courses in Singapore, Malaysia, Thailand, Indonesia, Vietnam, and Mauritius. Currently, we are the longest continuously-running NLP training and coaching institution in Asia, helping people turn knowledge into real transformation.

Since the start, we have dedicated ourselves to catalysing individuals and organisations to become their own powerful drivers of their envisioned success—through our strong emphasis on NLP, Enneagram Personality Profiling and other cutting-edge change technologies.

We believe the keys to successful training includes experiential and whole-brain integrated learning, and we have created our programmes around these important themes. We focus primarily on three connecting concepts: "brain-friendly", "hands-on", and "how to do it", so that clients fully integrate learning and success—in every facet of their lives.

MT Consulting (MTC) is the corporate arm of Mind Transformations serving corporate clients in the fields of coaching and experiential learning. We have a wide, diverse network of certified professionals and coaches and an active community to serve our clients. We aim to help organisations become VUCA-fit; support leaders to scale and future-proof; and develop employees to perform and transform.

Our Trainers, NLP, and Coaching Certification programmes are accepted or approved by:

- American Board of NLP (ABNLP)
- NLP University – Robert Dilts, United States
- International Association of Coaching Institutes (ICI)
- International Association of NLP Institutes (IN)
- International Enneagram Association (IEA)

Learn more about us and our programmes at: **https://www.mindtransformations.com/.**

ABOUT THE AUTHOR

Tang Seok Hian is the founder of IKIGAI Consultancy Services Pte Ltd, which specialises in organisation development, leadership training, and coaching. She is also the co-developer of the Neuro-Linguistic Enneagram (NLE) profiling tool (for individuals and teams), teaching and certifying practitioners to use the NLE tool and working with teams using the NLE Team profile.

With more than 25 years of HR and leadership experience and 17 years of practising Enneagram, Seok Hian now mostly applies Enneagram in leadership coaching, co-founders' relationship coaching, and team coaching. She also facilitates team workshops using the Enneagram and unlocks the team's ability to have deep conversations, alignment, and trust, thus helping teams optimise their team dynamics and drive performance.

www.ingramcontent.com/pod-product-compliance
Lightning Source LLC
LaVergne TN
LVHW010354160826
845677LV00005BA/1273

* 9 7 8 9 8 1 1 7 6 6 7 1 8 *